Sufism

A concise and widely acclaimed introduction to the fundamental doctrines and practices of Sufism, the inward or mystical dimension of Islam.

Other works by the same author:

Outline of Hinduism

Outline of Buddhism

Sufism

The Mystical Doctrines and Methods of Islam

by

William Stoddart

with a Foreword by
R. W. J. Austin
School of Oriental Studies, University of Durham

Paragon House
St. Paul, Minnesota

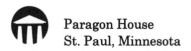

Published by Paragon House
2700 University Avenue West
St. Paul, Minnesota 55114

Second Printing

Revised Edition Copyright © 1985 by William
Stoddard
Original Edition © 1976 by William Stoddart
Published by the Aquarian Press, Wellborough,
Northamptonshire, England.

Revised Edition Copyright © 1985 by William Stod-
dard. Original Edition © 1976 by William Stoddart
Published by the Aquarian Press, Wellborough,
Northamptonshire, England.

ISBN: 0-913757-47-0

Library of Congress Cataloging in Publication Data

**Library of Congress Cataloging-in-Publication
Data**

Stoddart, William.
    Sufism : the mystical doctrines and methods of
Islam.

    Bibliography:
        Includes index.

    1. Sufism.   I. Title.
BP189.S74   1985   297'.4   85-16987
ISBN 0-913757-47-0 (pbk.)

To God belong the East and West. Wheresoe'er ye turn, there is the Face of God. Verily God is all-embracing and all-knowing.

Qur'ān, II, 115

Worship God as if thou sawest Him, for if thou seest Him not, verily He seeth thee.

The Prophet Muḥammad

CONTENTS

The Divine Name *(Allāh)*
surrounded by verses from the Qur'ān
(from a Moroccan woodcut)

ILLUSTRATIONS

FOREWORD

Few would today dispute that we live in an age marked, as few others have been, by a prevailing spiritual confusion and ambiguity. One of the principal effects of this state of affairs has been an unprecedented outpouring of the printed word on the subject of religion in general and mysticism in particular, which is a manifestation at once of a deep spiritual hunger and of the rampant mental curiosity so characteristic of secularized man.

However, since the outer forms and doctrines of established religion have become 'outmoded' and 'discredited' in this liberal age, the concern of many of the more recent exponents of religious wisdom has been to isolate the mystical, and therefore the apparently less formal, aspects of the major religious traditions and present them, out of context, as newly discovered 'philosophies for our times'. This practice of attempting to cream off from the major religions material considered acceptable and palatable to a secularized reading public is ill-conceived, deceptive and dangerous, since it leads people to imagine that they are able, without the necessary doctrinal and psychological training, to acquire the spiritual blessing and benefit intended only for those whose commitment is to the particular tradition as a whole.

This phenomenon is manifest in the many pseudo-oriental cults which now abound in the main urban centres of the Western world. Although, until recently, interest of this kind has been largely restricted to various aspects of Hindu and Buddhist spirituality, Sufism, the mystical tradition of Islam, has now also become an object of curiosity and re-adaptation, and this new book on Sufism is to be welcomed as a corrective to much muddled thinking on the subject.

There are various ways in which one may approach the study of Islamic mysticism. Firstly, there is the approach of the Sufi himself, who regards his Way or Method as the true expression of Islamic spirituality which, as such, began with the Prophet Muḥammad and has been part and parcel of the spiritual tradition of Islam as a whole ever since. To study Sufism from purely Sufi sources, however, assumes a thorough acquaintance with Islamic religion in general and also preferably a grasp of one of its native languages. Secondly, one may study the many works of scholarship produced over the last fifty years or so by Western orientalists, much of it painstaking and highly informative, but almost completely lacking in any appreciation of the experiential flavour of Sufism so essential for any proper understanding. Also, this approach is usually committed to the notion, variously expressed, that Sufism is something essentially alien to Islam which has been grafted onto it by borrowing from other religions.

Lastly, there is what may be termed the universalist approach, which regards Islam and Sufism as a particular manifestation of universal human aspirations towards the supernatural and spiritual. This approach can be extremely useful and illuminating, especially in these times, when an exposition of fundamental principles and symbols can guide the seeker through the profusion of religions and cults which are now offered to him. This is particularly true of the valuable work of such writers as Ananda Coomaraswamy, René Guénon and Frithjof Schuon who, while perceiving the spiritual essentials common to all the great religious traditions, do not make the mistake, so often made today, of belittling the significance and importance of a definite and unequivocal commitment to one particular tradition, nor do they forget the truth that the individual is moulded by a religious tradition and not vice versa.

For, just as the universalist approach can be of great help to present day seekers, it can, in the wrong hands, be extremely misleading, since there are two ways in which this approach can be misused. It is an approach often adopted by secular scholars, particularly anthropologists and sociologists, who tend to study all religions as universally primitive and outmoded attempts on the part of pre-scientific man to comprehend the universe and his place in it. In other words, they reject the validity and truth of all religions, except as interesting specimens for 'objective' scrutiny. A universalist approach is also adopted by the host of mystic cult pedlars who take refuge in a vague, blurring universalism in order to conceal their unwillingness to submit or commit themselves to the spiritual, mental and psychological obligations incumbent upon any genuine seeker after truth.

Dr Stoddart has produced a work on Sufism which provides the serious reader with a true universalist approach, in that he has kept firmly and distinctly in view the Islamic nature and context of Sufism, while employing comparisons with other religious traditions where such comparison illuminates common fundamental principles and does not obscure real and providential differences of spiritual perspective, a consideration of crucial importance in any legitimate study of the religions of the world.

R. W. J. Austin
School of Oriental Studies
University of Durham

ACKNOWLEDGEMENTS

The author wishes to thank the following for permission to reproduce the quotations and illustrations appearing in this book:

Titus Burckhardt for the quotation from his book *Fes, Stadt des Islam* and for illustration 7; Martin Lings, Allen & Unwin of London and Macmillan of New York for the quotation from *A Sufi Saint of the Twentieth Century;* the British Library Board for illustration 2; Jean-Louis Michon for illustration 3; James Dickie and the International Rumi Society for illustration 5.

AUTHOR'S NOTE

In the transliteration of Arabic words the most generally accepted method has been used throughout, with the following exceptions: *tā marbūta* has not been transliterated at all, except where a vowel follows, thus; *sūra*, but *Sūrat aḍ-Ḍuḥā* (or *Sūratu 'ḍ-Ḍuḥā*); likewise the terminal *hamza* has not been transliterated except where a vowel follows, thus: *fanā*, but *fanā' al-fanā* (or *fanā'u 'l-fanā'i*).

As regards the pronunciation of the words 'exoterism' and 'esoterism' (used throughout the book), let it be said that the emphasis falls on the second syllable. These forms have been preferred to the alternatives 'exotericism' and 'esotericism' in which, as in the adjectives 'exoteric' and 'esoteric', the emphasis falls on the third syllable.

INTRODUCTION

No Sufism without Islam

Sufism is the spirituality or mysticism of the religion of Islam. Mysticism makes its appearance, as an inward dimension, in every religion, and to attempt to separate the mystical element from the religion which is its outward support is an arbitrary act of violence which cannot but be fatal to the mysticism, or spiritual path, concerned. In the present century, however, the attempt to do precisely this has been made repeatedly, and time and time again we are offered a Vedanta (or a yoga) without Hinduism, or a Zen (or something purporting to be such) without Buddhism.

In recent times nothing has suffered more from this vain procedure than Sufism: in a variety of forms and in many parts of the Western world we are now offered a Sufism without Islam! One might as well try to purvey human life without a human body! To be sure, the body (though made in the image of God) is corruptible and mortal, while life is invisible and immortal. Nevertheless, as far as we in this world are concerned, it is only in the body that life finds its support and expression. So is it also in the case of mysticism or spirituality: this is the inward or supra-formal dimension, of which the respective religion is the outward or formal expression. One cannot be a Benedictine without being a Christian, or a Sufi without being a Muslim. There is no Sufism without Islam.

Exoterism and esoterism

In Islam the two domains – outward and inward – remain more or less distinct, though they bear a very definite relationship to one another. This relationship can perhaps best be described as follows: the outward religion, or 'exoterism', (known in Islam as the *sharī'a*), may be likened to the circumference of a circle. The inner Truth, or 'esoterism', that lies at the heart of the religion (and is known in Islam as *ḥaqīqa*), may be likened to the circle's centre. The radius proceeding from circumference to centre represents the mystical or 'initiatic' path *(ṭarīqa)* that leads from outward observance to inner conviction, from belief to vision, from potency to act.

In Arabic, Sufism is called *taṣawwuf*. Both words come from *ṣūf* ('wool'), a reference to the woollen robe worn by the earliest Sufis. Since early times some have also linked the word *ṣufī* with *ṣūfiya* ('purified' or 'chosen as a friend [by God]'). The connection with the Greek *sophia* ('wisdom'), however, is generally regarded as no more than a pious pun, since the Greek letter *sigma* is regularly transliterated by the Arabic letter *sīn*, and not by *ṣād* as in *ṣūfi*. It is interesting to note, however, that in much later times, the Turks transliterated Hagia Sophia (the Church of the Holy Wisdom in Istanbul) as *Aya Ṣūfiya*, replacing here the Greek *sigma* with the letter *ṣād*.[1]

Strictly speaking, the Arabic word *ṣūfī*, like the Sanskrit word *yogi*, refers only to one who has attained the goal; nevertheless, it is often applied by extension

[1] For a full discussion of this question, see 'The Necessity for the Rise of the Term Ṣūfī' by Victor Danner in *Studies in Comparative Religion*, London, Spring 1972.

to initiates who are still merely travelling towards it. The word 'initiate' serves to indicate that, in order to embark on the spiritual path, a special rite of initiation is an indispensable prerequisite. More will be said about this later.

From the foregoing it will be seen that Sufism *(taṣawwuf)* comprises both esoterism and initiation, *ḥaqīqa* and *ṭarīqa*, doctrine and method.

The *sharī'a*, for its part, is the 'outward' religion which is accessible to, and indispensable for, *all*. *Taṣawwuf*, on the other hand, is only for those possessed of the necessary vocation. In practice, therefore, it cannot but be the affair of a minority, though it may sometimes have popular manifestations.

Classification of the religions

For certain historical and other reasons, Hinduism and Buddhism are more familiar to Westerners than is Islam. It is not simply that Islam is misunderstood: it is that people are much more ignorant of it than of any other non-Christian religion. Islam might almost be called 'the unknown religion'. In view of this, it may be useful to digress for a moment from our main theme, and consider the classification of the religions, so that, before we go any further, Islam's place amongst them may be better understood.

Firstly, one may look at the religions from a simple geographical point of view. The religion of the Far East is, predominantly, Buddhism – *Mahayana* (or 'Great Vehicle') in Tibet, China and Japan, and *Theravada* (or 'Primitive Way') in Ceylon, Burma, Siam and Cambodia. In the Indian sub-continent, the predominant religion, covering three-quarters of the total population, is Hinduism. In the Middle East, Near East and North Africa, as well as parts of the Indian sub-continent, the religion of the overwhelming majority is Islam. (In this connection, however, one must never forget the 'Yellow'[2] Islam of Malaya and Indonesia, and the 'Black'[2] Islam of Africa south of the Sahara.) In Europe, of course, the religion is Christianity: Orthodoxy, largely, in the East, and Catholicism, largely, in the West.

From a somewhat deeper point of view, one may look at the religions according to their *type*. Thus we have the diverse branches of Hyperborean shamanism: Taoism, Shinto, Bön (the pre-Buddhist religion of Tibet), Siberian shamanism, and the religion of the North American Indians; then we have the Aryan mythologies: Hinduism, Buddhism, Jainism, Zoroastrianism, and the now extinct Greco-Roman, Nordic and Celtic religions; and finally we have the Semitic monotheisms (ultimately stemming from Abraham): Judaism, Christianity and Islam.

The latter is probably the most useful of the classifications; but there are certain relationships which cross the frontiers of the categories mentioned. Thus Buddhism, Christianity and Islam are 'universal' religions, claiming the allegiance of peoples everywhere, while Hinduism and Judaism are both the religions of a single people (or group of peoples). Then again, Hinduism and Christianity have a link in that they are both 'incarnationist', and thus modify, in this respect, the 'strict' monotheism of Judaism and Islam. Buddhism, for its part, enjoys the distinction of being the only 'non-theistic' religion – not

[2] These terms are used solely to designate the race of the peoples concerned, and have no other significance.

atheistic, of course, since like the other religions it is based on the idea of a transcendent Absolute (called, in Buddhism, Nirvana or Buddhahood).

In summary, then, we see that Islam, while being located principally in the Near East and North Africa, is 'universal'; it is also Semitic (i.e. one of the three religions deriving from Abraham); and finally, far from being 'incarnationist', it is strictly monotheistic. Notwithstanding Sikhism (to which a reference will be made later), it is also the youngest of all the religious revelations.

Another highly important feature that characterizes the religions is their point of view regarding the 'equality' or 'inequality' of men.

Mankind may be looked at either from the point of view of its differentiation or from that of its equality. The hierarchical differentiation of mankind finds expression in Hinduism (with its four castes: *brahmins*, *kshatriyas*, *vaishyas*, *shudras*) and in Christianity (with its four estates: Lords Spiritual, Lords Temporal, craftsmen and merchants, serfs). From this point of view, men are manifestly unequal, and hierarchy goes hand in hand with heredity. The purpose of heredity is precisely the preservation – or perpetuation – of quality. Not only the colour of one's eyes, but also intelligence and character depend on birth. With the privileges of birth, be it noted in passing, go obligations. *Noblesse oblige.* Islam, on the other hand, is based on human equality. This shows itself both positively and negatively: firstly, man's 'theomorphic' nature is common to all, and secondly, the wretchedness of man's terrestrial exile is shared by prince and commoner alike: all human beings are inescapably faced with suffering, and all human beings must die. Buddhism also takes this point of view. Equality is thus as inherent to mankind as is hierarchy; and one, just as much as the other, may be the basis of a religious perspective.

No matter which of the two predominates in a given religion, however, the other is also implicitly and actually present. Thus in Christianity it is fundamental that *all* are 'created in the image of God'; and in Hinduism, no one asks the *sannyasin* his caste. In Islam, on the other hand, the reality of heredity finds expression in the existence of the *shurafā* or descendents of the Prophet. These possess no specific 'caste' function, but enjoy certain inherent spiritual advantages.

Finally we may note that, whereas Hinduism is the oldest of the religions, Islam is the youngest.

CHAPTER ONE

THE RELIGION OF ISLAM

Islam is the third of the three Semitic monotheisms. It has its origin in the revelation which the Prophet Muḥammad – scion of a noble Arab tribe (the Quraish) settled in seventh-century Mecca – received from God through the intermediary of the Archangel Gabriel. This revelation came upon Muḥammad when he was in middle life, and he made it known progressively to his companions over a number of years. These intermittent utterances of the revelation were subsequently committed to writing, and constitute the Qur'ān,[1] the sacred book of Islam. For Islam, the Qur'ān is the direct and immediate Word of God.

The language of the Qur'ān is Arabic, which is the sacred language of Islam. As such, it occupies an even more fundamental position in Islam than do the various liturgical languages (Latin, Greek, Slavonic, etc.) in Christianity. Its role is more comparable to that of Sanskrit in Hinduism or Hebrew in Judaism. It is significant that Arabic is the most archaic of all the living Semitic languages: its morphology is to be found in Hammurabi's code which is more or less contemporary with Abraham.[2] The words of the Qur'ān have been faithfully preserved in the form in which they were originally received, even down to the minutest points

[1] *Qur'ān* is the Arabic for 'recitation'.

[2] Cf. Édouard Dhorme, *Mélanges Louis Massignon*, Damascus, 1957. (See Titus Burckhardt's 'Arab or Islamic Art?' in *Studies in Comparative Religion*, London, Winter 1971.)

of detail, and their recitation constitutes a 'liturgical' act. For this purpose only the original Arabic may be used, as translations have no liturgical validity.

Being the 'uncreated Word of God', it is the Qur'ān, and not Muḥammad, which is at the centre of the Islamic religion. This contrasts outwardly with Christianity, where it is Christ, and not the New Testament, who is at the centre. This contrast is purely outward, however, as in Christianity Christ is, precisely, the 'uncreated Word of God', and thus, in this respect, there is a far-reaching inward analogy. Herein lies the reason why an adherent of Christianity (which is centred on Christ) is called a 'Christian', whereas an adherent of Islam (which is not, in the first instance, centred on Muhammad) is not properly designated by the term 'Muhammadan',[3] but is called a 'Muslim'. 'Muslim' means 'one who submits' and 'Islam' means 'submission' (i.e. to God).

In Christianity, Christ is 'true Man and true God'. Using the same terminology, one could say that in Islam Muḥammad is 'true Man' only. As we have seen, it is the Qur'ān and not Muḥammad, that is divine. As Frithjof Schuon has pointed out, the role of Muḥammad in Islam is in some ways analogous to that of the Virgin Mary in Christianity.[4] The annunciation to Mary, like the revelation to Muḥammad, came through the Archangel Gabriel. Mary, a virgin, produced a Son, while Muḥammad, 'un-lettered' *(ummī)*, produced a Book. Muḥammad's 'illiteracy', like Mary's virginity, is of profound metaphysical and spiritual significance.

[3] The term 'Muhammadan' does have a role, and means simply 'of Muḥammad' or 'pertaining to Muḥammad'.

[4] See *The Transcendent Unity of Religions* (Harper & Row, New York, 2nd edition, 1975).

Though Muḥammad is viewed simply as a man, he is no ordinary man. Muslims speak of him as a 'jewel amongst stones', rather as Christians say *benedicta tu in mulieribus* of Mary.

At another level, of course, there is an obvious analogy between Muḥammad and Christ, as each is the founder and 'revealer' of the respective religion. And, very characteristically, Muḥammad's role as revealer and legislator is a strongly masculine one.

*

* *

When one speaks of the 'Semitic monotheisms' (Judaism, Christianity, Islam), one is contrasting them, as was explained in the Introduction, with the 'Aryan mythologies', such as Hinduism and Buddhism. Following its revelation to Muḥammad, Islam rapidly spread to become the religion of virtually all Arabs. Both Jews and Arabs, as Semitic peoples, belong to the posterity of Abraham, but whereas the Jews trace their descent from Isaac,[5] son of Abraham and Sarah, the Arabs (including Muḥammad) are descended from Ishmael, the son of Abraham and Hagar. Indeed the Ka'ba at Mecca was built by Abraham and Ishmael. Thus for Islam, Ishmael plays a cardinal and prophetic role.

As for Christianity, it was the 'Gentile' (or Aryan) Europeans who were destined to embrace it and thereby to become spiritually 'semiticized' – though never entirely losing a certain Aryan cast of spirit deriving from classical antiquity and moulded also by their Indo-European languages. A number of other Aryan peoples, such as the Persians and many Indians, were spiritually

[5] Isaac's son Jacob could be said to be the first Jew.

semiticized by their conversion to the religion of the Arab Prophet. In India, for example, the spiritual and psychological difference between the Aryan Hindus and the spiritually semiticized Muslims (even when both belong to the selfsame Aryan race) is marked.

*

* *

In the next chapter the point will be made that, contrary to the view of some orientalists, Sufism is in principle entirely orthodox. The concept of orthodoxy in general is one which, in our day, is far from being properly understood. It can be approached from two directions: firstly, it represents conformity to the religion as it was revealed;[6] secondly, it represents conformity to truth as such. The two senses do not in principle conflict, as the revelation is itself an expression of the truth (albeit an expression destined to meet the circumstances of a specific time and place) and orthodoxy is, as it were, the principle of truth running through the myths, symbols and dogmas which are the very language of revelation. Contrariwise, heresy can be viewed, either as a departure from the religion as revealed, or else as a departure from truth pure and simple. Seen in this way, the 'dogmas' of a religion are not the intellectual prisons that they are often assumed to be, but doorways which, when fully penetrated spiritually, open to a literally unlimited intellectual freedom.

Another way of looking at it is this: even in the circumstances of today, many people still preserve the

[6] Adherence to the religion as revealed does not, of course, preclude any legitimate development or adaptation of the revelation in view of particular circumstances.

notion of 'moral purity' and lay high value on it. Orthodoxy is 'doctrinal purity', purity in the realm of knowledge. As such, it clearly is of primary importance. Moreover, it is an indispensable condition for any interreligious dialogue. The reason for this has been well explained by Bernard Kelly:

> Confusion is inevitable whenever cultures based on profoundly different spiritual traditions intermingle without rigid safeguards to preserve their purity. The crusader with the cross emblazoned on his breast, the loincloth and spindle of Mahatma Gandhi when he visited Europe, are images of the kind of precaution that is reasonable when travelling in a spiritually alien territory. The modern traveller in his bowler hat and pin-stripes is safeguarded by that costume against any lack of seriousness in discussing finance. Of more important safeguards he knows nothing. The complete secularism of the modern western world, wherever its influence has spread, has opened the flood-gates to a confusion which sweeps away the contours of the spirit. . . . Traditional norms . . . provide the criteria of culture and civilization. Traditional orthodoxy is thus the prerequisite of any discourse at all between the traditions themselves.[7]

*

* *

The monumental differences between modern civilization and what remains of the traditional civilizations (including that of Islam) are well known to travellers, and even to Europeans who have merely read about the latter. A child of his time and a victim of his mental limitations, the average European experiences considerable feelings of superiority at the contrast, and has for the most part nothing but contempt for those

[7] *Dominican Studies*, Vol. 7, 1954, p. 256.

manifestations of traditional civilization that are known to him. Some people, consciously or unconsciously, assume that modern civilization exemplifies some essential aspect of Christianity and believe, for that reason, that Christianity simply must be superior to the other religions. In the comparative study of the religions, no greater error is possible!

Modern civilization has its origins in the Renaissance, that great inrush of secularization, when nominalism vanquished realism, individualism (or humanism) replaced universalism, and empiricism banished scholasticism. The principles lying behind the genesis and nature of modern civilization were lucidly set forth in a remarkable series of works, published in the earlier part of this century, by René Guénon, who was also a masterly exponent of the metaphysics and symbolism of all the religions.[8] An even richer and more far-reaching exposition of religion and metaphysics (coupled with a penetrating critique of modern civilization) has come, in the second part of this century, from Frithjof Schuon.[9] The same perspective was brilliantly represented in the English-speaking world in the later writings of Ananda Coomaraswamy.[10] Amongst other things these authors demonstrated that there is a perfect spiritual equivalence between pre-Renaissance (or Medieval) Christianity and the various oriental religions. In other words, while the civiliza-

[8] See especially his books *The Crisis of the Modern World* (Luzac, London) and *The Reign of Quantity and the Signs of the Times* (Penguin Books, Baltimore, Md.).

[9] In addition to those of his books mentioned on other pages, see *Esoterism as Principle and as Way* (World Wisdom Books, Bloomington, Indiana, 1981); *Castes and Races* (Perennial Books, Bedfont, England, 1981); and *The Writings of Frithjof Schuon: a Basic Reader* (Crossroad, New York, 1985).

[10] See *The Bugbear of Literacy* (Perennial Books, Bedfont, England, 1979) and *Figures of Speech, Figures of Thought* (Luzac, London, 1946). The latter book, which is perhaps his finest work, was reprinted virtually in its entirety in *Coomaraswamy: Selected Papers, Volume 2,* edited by Roger Lipsey (Princeton University Press, 1977).

tion of Christendom was still traditional, it was entirely analogous to the traditional civilizations of the Orient. There is no continuity whatsoever between the spirit that gave rise to modern civilization and the Christian tradition. When, therefore, in these pages, any comparison is made between Christianity and Islam (or between Christian mysticism and Sufism) it is naturally traditional or Medieval Christianity that is intended.

*

* *

As has already been mentioned, the ultimate source of the Islamic religion is the Qur'ān, revealed to the Prophet Muḥammad. A secondary source of Muslim doctrine and practice is the Wont (*Sunna*) of the Prophet. The *Sunna* includes not only the customs and usages, but also the Sayings (or Traditions) of the Prophet (*aḥadīth,* sing. *ḥadīth*). The latter are a cardinal source of Muslim teaching. A particularly important type of *ḥadīth* is the *ḥadīth qudsī* in which God Himself speaks through the mouth of the Prophet. Such sayings, although of Divine inspiration, are distinct from the Quranic revelation.

The *Sunna* constitutes a norm for the whole of Islamic civilization. Love of the Prophet (who is usually referred to as the 'Messenger of God', *Rasūlu'Llāh*) is much cultivated in Islam, and classically takes the form of conformity to his *Sunna* or Wont.

The central Message (*risāla*) of Islam is the declaration of faith (*shahāda*): 'There is no god but God; Muḥammad is the Messenger of God.' (*Lā ilāha illā 'Llāh: Muḥammadur Rasūlu 'Llāh.*) All Muslim doctrine and, above all, Sufi doctrine, derives from the *shahāda.*

The Islamic Law or *sharīʿa* is characterized by the 'Five Pillars (*arkām*) of Islam'. These are faith, prayer, fasting, almsgiving and pilgrimage. Faith (*īmān*) is assent to the *shahāda*. Prayer (*ṣalāt*) is the canonical prayer that is observed five times daily (at dawn, noon, afternoon, sunset and night). Fasting (*ṣawm*) is the abstention from food and drink from dawn to sunset observed during the month of Ramaḍān. Almsgiving (*zakāt*) is the giving of one's goods for charitable purposes. Pilgrimage (*ḥajj*) is the pilgrimage to the Kaʿba at Mecca which a Muslim should make, if possible, at least once in his lifetime. As we shall see in Chapter 3, Sufism adds to the literal meaning of each of the Five Pillars a metaphysical and spiritual interpretation.

In addition to the Five Pillars of Islam, one should also mention the well-known Muslim prohibition of wine and pork. Wine is a 'good' thing in itself, as is proved by the fact that it is promised the faithful in Paradise, and also by the positive use which many Sufis have made of the imagery of wine and drunkenness to symbolize mystical states.[11] In its negative aspect, however, it is the symbol of confusion or error. Pork is the symbol of uncleanness or sin. In the Semitic perspective it has no positive symbolism, although it should be noted that the wild boar is not covered by the prohibition. Gambling and usury are also forbidden by Islamic law. An interesting sidelight on Islamic attitudes is provided by the fact that it is forbidden to men to wear gold or silk. These two precious substances are reserved for the use of women.

Another well known Islamic concept is that of the 'holy war'(*jiād*). Outwardly, this refers to the defence of the Islamic community. Inwardly or spiritually, it refers to the unseen warfare against the ego. The Prophet indicated the relation-

[11] Likewise wine appears at the centre of Chrisian worship as the 'blood of Christ'.

ship of these two aspects of the holy war when he remarked to his companions following a battle: 'We are returning from the lesser holy war (against our outward enemies), to the greater holy war (against ourselves)!'

1. The Kaʿba at Mecca
(from a sixteenth-century set of tiles)

Islam accepts, and incorporates into itself, all antecedent prophets of Abrahamic lineage, up to and including Jesus and Mary.[12] There are more references in the Qur'ān to the Virgin Mary (Sayyidat-nā Maryam) than in the New Testament. One of its chapters is even called after her. As for Jesus (Sayyid-nā 'Īsā), he is often called the 'Seal of Sanctity' *(khātim al-wilaya)*. The term 'Seal of Prophecy' *(khātim an-nubuwwa)* is reserved for Muḥammad. Jesus and Mary play a certain inward role in the spiritual economy of Sufism. This is particularly apparent in the lives and works of such great Sufis as Muhyi 'd-Dīn ibn 'Arabī and Manṣūr al-Ḥallāj.

*

* *

The only imporant 'division' within Islam is that between Sunnis and Shī'is. Orthodox (Sunni) Islam recognizes that the immediate successors *(khalīfas)* to the Prophet Muḥammad, as head of the Islamic community, are the four Caliphs, Abu Bakr, Omar, Othman and 'Alī. The establishment and subsequent development of Islam as a world religion rests on the pattern set by these four holy patriarchs. Shī'ism, on the contrary, rejects the first three Caliphs and regards the fourth Caliph 'Alī as the only legitimate immediate successor to the Prophet, the chief reason being that 'Alī was of the 'family of the Prophet', since he was the latter's son-in-law.

[12] An implicit recognition of the Prophets of the non-Semitic religions is to be found in the Quranic verse: 'Verily we have sent Messengers before thee (Muḥammad). About some of them We have told thee, *and about some of them We have not told thee.*' (*Sura of the Believer*, 78). The Qur'ān also says: 'For every community there is a Messenger.' (*Sura of Jonah*, 47).

The name Shī'a (the general term for Shī'is) comes from *shī'atu 'Ali*, 'the party of 'Alī'. Though 'schismatical' from the Sunni point of view, Shī'ism retains virtually all the orthodox doctrines and practices of Islam – apart, of course, from the major matter of rejecting the first three Caliphs. By diverging thus from official Islam, Shī'ism has developed a characteristic religious climate of its own – one which can be witnessed in Persia (where Shī'is predominate) and the other scattered areas where Shī'is are to be found. The great Sufi poets of Persia, however, such as Jalāl ad-Dīn Rūmī and Omar Khayyam were Sunnis.[13]

*
* *

From the time of the Crusades many Christians have considered Islam, bordering as it does on Christendom, to be a threat and rival to the latter. And yet Islam's record towards Christianity is a good one, and its age-old tolerance of Christian and Jewish communities ('People of the Book', *ahl al-kitāb*) living in its midst is well known. Islam's attitude to Christianity has its root in the Qur'ān: 'You will find that the best friends of believers are those who say: "We are Christians". This is because there are priests and monks amongst them, and because they are not proud.' (*Sura of the Table Spread*, 85).

A modern testimony regarding one part of the Muslim world comes from a Catholic missionary: 'One can safely say . . . that in Africa's Moslem millions there

[13] For a penetrating evaluation of the Shī'a schism, see 'The Seeds of a Divergence' by Frithjof Schuon in *Islam and the Perennial Philosophy* (World of Islam Festival Publishing Company, London, 1976).

is a great fund of sincere religious sentiment and of goodwill towards non-Moslems.'[14] The late Sir Abubakar Tafewa Balewa of Nigeria, on receiving a message of blessing from Pope Pius XII, kept the Bishops who presented it to him standing while he read and re-read the message, with tears flowing from his eyes.

Many of the Scholastic philosophers knew and valued the works of Islamic theologians. Dante used Islamic sources in the *Divine Comedy*. In more modern times, Pope Pius XI in despatching his Apostolic Delegate to Libya, said to him: 'Do not think you are going amongst infidels. Muslims attain to Salvation. The ways of God are infinite.'[15] Pope Pius XII remarked how consoling it was to know that, all over the world, there were millions of people who, five times a day, bow down before God. Not long ago the Catholic Bishops of Nigeria, in the concluding words of a joint Pastoral Letter, afforded a good example of a just Christian attitude towards Islam: 'We express sentiments of fraternal love towards our Muslim fellow-citizens. . . . We appreciate their deep spirit of prayer and fasting. . . . We are united against tendencies towards materialism and secularism.'[16]

*

*   *

It cannot be said too often that the religion of Islam stems entirely from the Qur'ān. One of its translators, Marmaduke Pickthall, called it 'that inimitable symphony, the very sounds of which move men to tears and

[14] Fr. Patrick O'Connor, *Catholic Herald*, 9 January 1959.

[15] *L'Ultima* (Florence), VIII, 1954.

[16] *Catholic Herald*, 21 October 1960.

ecstasy.' In order to let the reader taste a little of the flavour of the Qur'ān as directly as possible, this chapter will end with two characteristic passages, firstly in the original Arabic, and then in English translation.

Inna 'l-muslimīna wa 'l-muslimāti
wa 'l-mu'minīna wa 'l-mu'mināti
wa 'l-qānitīna wa 'l-qānitāti
wa 'ṣ-ṣādiqīna wa 'ṣ-ṣādiqāti
wa 'ṣ-ṣābirīna wa 'ṣ-ṣabirāti
wa 'l-khāshi'īna wa 'l-khāshi'āti
wa 'l-mutaṣaddiqīna wa 'l-mutaṣaddiqāti
wa 'ṣ-ṣā'imina wa 'ṣ-ṣā'imāti
wa 'l-ḥāfizīna furūja-hum wa 'l-ḥāfizāti
wa 'dh-dhārkirīna 'Llāha kathīran wa 'dh-dhākirāti
ā' adda 'Llāhu la-hum maghfiratan wa ajran 'azīman
Sūrat al-Aḥzāb, 35

Verily men who submit [to God] and women who submit,
and men who believe and women who believe,
and men who are devout and women who are devout,
and men who speak the truth and women who speak the truth,
and men who are patient and women who are patient,
and men who are humble and women who are humble,
and men who give alms and women who give alms,
and men who fast and women who fast,
and men who guard their modesty and women who guard,
and men who remember God much and women who remember,
God has prepared for them forgiveness and a vast reward.
Sura of the Confederates, 35

Wa 'ḍ-ḍuhā,
wa 'l-laili idhā sajā,
mā wadda'a-ka rabbu-ka wa mā qalā,
wa la 'l-akhiratu khairun la-ka min al-ūlā,
wa la-saufa yu'ṭī-ka rabbu-ka fa-tarḍā
a lam yajid-ka yatīman fa-awā?
Wa wajada-ka ḍallan fa-hadā?
Wa wajada-ka 'ā'ilan fa-aghnā?
Fa-ammā 'l-yatīma fa-lā taqhar,
wa ammā 's-sā'ila fa-lā tanhar,
wa ammā bi-ni'mati rabbi-ka fa-ḥaddith.

Sūrat aḍ-Ḍuḥā

By the brightness of day,
and by the night when it covereth,
thy Lord hath not forsaken thee nor doth He hate thee,
and verily the next world will be better for thee than this one,
and verily thy Lord will give unto thee so that thou wilt be content.
Did He not find thee an orphan and protect thee?
Did He not find thee wandering and direct thee?
Did He not find thee destitute and enrich thee?
Therefore the orphan oppress not,
therefore the beggar turn not away,
therefore of the bounty of Thy Lord be thy discourse.

Sura of the Brightness of Day

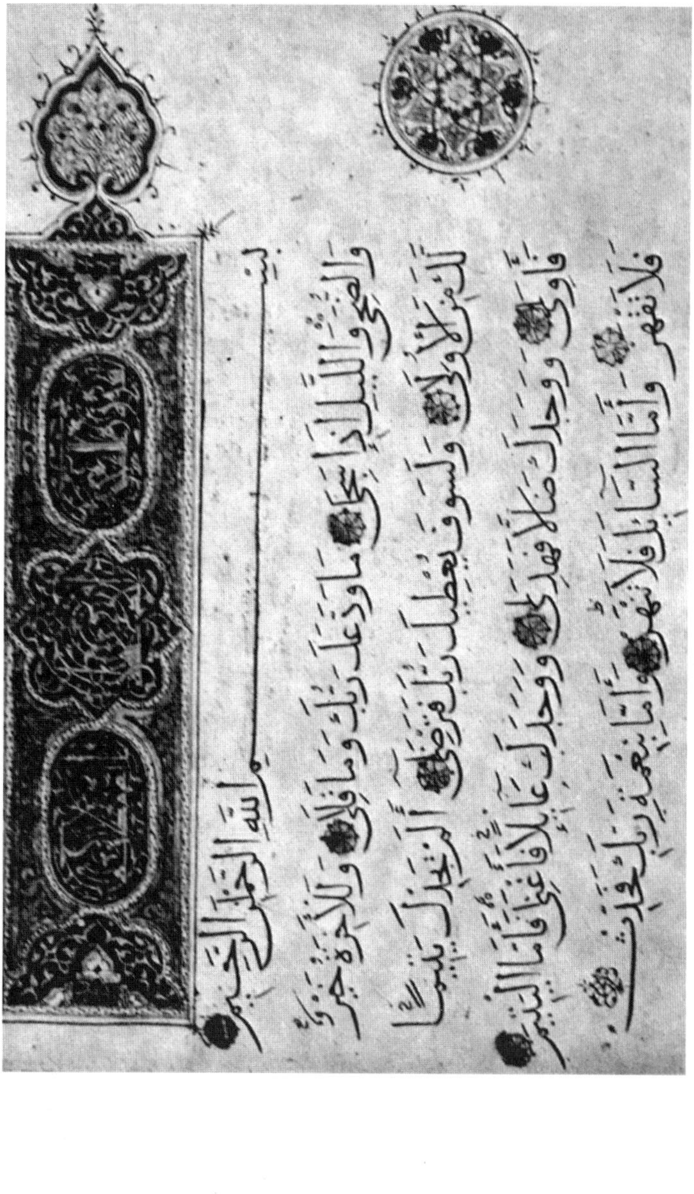

2. The Sura of the Brightness of Day (*Sūrat aḍ-Ḍuḥā*)
(from a thirteenth-century Near-Eastern Qur'ān)

CHAPTER TWO

ISLAMIC ESOTERISM

This chapter will be concerned chiefly with the doctrinal side of *ḥaqīqa* – the name given to the 'inner Truth' or 'inner Reality' that is at the heart of the Islamic revelation. The *sharī'a* (outward law) is in fact the vehicle or expression of the *ḥaqīqa*, and this is why Sufis are always amongst the most ardent defenders of the outward law. This represents a paradox for those who, for various reasons, consider Sufism to be unorthodox, and a departure, precisely, from the orthodox *sharī'a*.

The explanation is that Sufism, while outwardly conforming, is inwardly free. The *sharī'a* is the doorway that opens on to freedom, the 'strait path that leadeth unto life'. For the Sufi, the 'doorway' is not an end in itself. Nevertheless, it remains venerable, and Christian doctrine (as expressed by St Paul) puts a much more extreme edge on the matter when it contrasts 'the letter that killeth' and 'the spirit that giveth life'.

It would have been impossible, however, for this inward freedom of Sufism never to have shown itself in a form which appeared to conflict with Islamic orthodoxy. There is the famous case of Al-Ḥallāj who, having in mind the doctrine of Unity (and above all having himself 'realized' man's essential identity with the Divine Principle and so transcended the distinction between 'slave' and 'Lord'), declared: 'I am the Truth' *(anā 'l-Ḥaqq)* – a declaration which earned him martyrdom at the hands of the 'exoteric' authorities.

A freedom which is total will always scandalize those who see no further than the outward limits, and there is even, objectively, from a certain point of view at least, a relationship of opposition between the 'inwardly informal' and the 'outwardly formal'. Meister Eckhart has said: 'If thou wouldst reach the kernel, thou must break the shell.'

The total freedom in respect of outward forms enjoyed by Sufis of a high degree of spiritual realization does not always lead to martyrdom, however, but sometimes to the most audacious *jeux d'esprit.* What a subtlety of interrelationships is betokened in the following story. The voice of God spoke to the Sufi Abū 'l-Ḥasan al-Kharraqānī,[1] saying: 'Shall I tell the people of thy "state" [i.e. his "spiritual drunkenness" or high degree of spiritual realization involving independence of outward forms], so that [being scandalized] they will stone thee?' Abū 'l-Ḥasan's state was such that he immediately answered back: 'Shall I tell the people of Thine infinite Mercy, so that they will never again bow down to Thee in prayer?'[2] Therein lies hidden the key to the relationship between exoterism and esoterism!

In summary, let it be said that Sufism cannot be other than orthodox, and this for two reasons: firstly, being the 'inward' dimension of the 'outward' dogma, it cannot repudiate the latter, though it 'frees' itself from the formal constraints of the dogma 'from within'. Secondly – and this is a point worth stressing – the doc-

[1] A Persian of the eleventh century.

[2] Such daring is not limited to Islam. The coach in which St Theresa of Avila was once travelling ran into a ditch. As she was extricating herself with some difficulty, she heard a voice saying: 'Dost thou not know, Theresa, that this is how I treat My friends?' St Theresa did not hesitate to answer back: 'It is small wonder, then, that Thou hast so few of them!'

trines and practices of Sufism, as Louis Massignon and other orientalists have amply demonstrated, are entirely derivable from the Qur'ān alone, the Qur'ān being the very basis of Islamic orthodoxy.

This latter fact specifically refutes the allegation that Sufism developed chiefly as a result of influences from extraneous sources such as Neo-Platonism, Christianity, or the Indian religions. Sufism has sometimes borrowed formulations deriving from Neo-Platonic and other spiritual doctrines which coincide with its own view of reality, but this has always been for convenience of expression, and does not constitute any syncretism.

*

* *

The central doctrine of Sufism is *waḥdat al-wujūd*, the 'oneness of being'. This is derived directly from the *shahāda*, which is understood not only as 'there is no god but God' but also as 'there is no reality except Reality'. One of the Names of God, indeed, is *al-Ḥaqq*, which means 'Reality' or 'Truth'.

The Sufis teach that the relative has no reality other than in the Absolute, and the finite has no reality other than in the Infinite. In Islam, man has access to the Absolute and the Infinite through the Qur'ān, which is the revelation of God to the world, and also through the Prophet who, within the world itself, is God's very reflection. The content of the Qur'ān, like the message of the Prophet, is essentially *lā ilāha illā 'Llāh, Muḥammadur Rasūlu 'Llāh*. In these two revealed and sacred clauses of the *shahāda*, man has access, on the one hand, to the Divine Immutability and, on the other, to the 'Muhammadan' or Prophetic Norm.

Muslims are known as 'the people of *lā ilāha illā 'Llāh*', and Sufis draw the full spiritual consequences from this their most precious possession. In and through the *shahāda* (with its dual reference to the Divinity and the Prophet), the imperfect is overwhelmed by the Perfect (the 'Muhammadan' Norm) and the impermanent is extinguished by the Permanent (God Himself). 'Say: Truth hath come and falsehood hath vanished away. Verily falsehood is ever bound to vanish.' (*Sura of the Children of Israel*, 81)

There is no 'duality' in the *shahāda*, however. The second clause, referring to the Prophet, is implicitly contained in the first. Frithjof Schuon has indicated how it logically derives from the word *illā*, 'except'.[3] Nevertheless, the Prophet's role is indispensable for man, as it is only through the Prophet, God's representative, that man may come to God Himself.

Nor is there any multiplicity in the first clause of the *shahāda:* It can be reduced to one word: *Allāh*, for, precisely, 'there is no god but God'!

Though here we are dealing only with doctrine (and not with 'spiritual realization' which is the subject of the next chapter, 'The Mystical Path'), it can be seen at once that Sufi doctrine is invariably 'operative'. That is to say, it is not merely theory, but a path *(ṭarīqa)* to be followed, as well as a tangible blessing *(baraka)* which acts as a viaticum.

Titus Burckhardt sums up the essential features of Sufism as follows:

> Possessing as it does the dual aspects of wisdom and the love of God, [Sufism] finds its expression not only in the

[3] *Understanding Islam* (Allen & Unwin, London, 1963, and Penguin Books, Baltimore, U.S.A., 1972), p. 126.

mental forms of metaphysics but also in poetry and the visual arts, and, as its essence is communicated most directly in symbols and analogies, it can speak without hindrance not only to learned believers, but also to the simple man of the people: the craftsman and the Bedouin; in fact, it may often be received more easily by the unlearned than by the learned.

Though Islamic mysticism, as it persists . . . down to the present day, may be compared in many respects with Christian mysticism – and in other respects with Hindu and Far-Eastern mysticism – it is nevertheless founded entirely on the religious form specific to Islam. Its point of departure is *Tawhīd*, the doctrine of Divine Unity. If Islamic law demands as the first duty of every believer, that he 'witness' the Unity of God, Islamic mysticism requires that this witness *(shahāda)* should not merely be a form of lip service, nor even a mental assent, but that it should be, beyond all reflections and sentiments, a total and immediate act of witness *(shahāda)*; 'witness' such as this means nothing other than the knowledge of God.

God can only be known, however, when the human ego, which instinctively regards itself as a self-sufficient centre – a kind of 'divinity' in addition to the Divinity – is extinguished before the infinitude of God, in accordance with the words: 'There is no divinity but God'. This does not mean that the immortal essence of the soul has to be annihilated; what must be dissolved is that mental morass, compounded of ego-determined passions and imaginings, the constant tendency of which is to restrict consciousness to the level of ephemeral appearances. When this 'veil' of selfishness is lifted from the Spirit which is hidden underneath – the Spirit which sees through to the essences of things – then for the first time things are seen as they really are. God is seen in His all-embracing Presence, and the creature as a pure possibility contained in the Divine Being.

The organ by means of which man takes cognizance of

the presence of God is, according to Sufi teaching, not the brain but the heart. As with the Christian Fathers, the heart is the seat, not of the sentiments, but of the Intellect or Spirit (*ar-Rūḥ*), which penetrates to Reality and transcends mental forms.

Deflected from the true centre of his being, which has its roots in the Eternal, the consciousness of the average man is as if imprisoned in a kind of dream or state of forgetfulness (*ghafla*). This is why man must be 'reminded' (of That which he has 'forgotten'), and this is the reason for what is known as *dhikr*, which the Sufi must practise in a large variety of ways, and which means 'recollection' or 'mindfulness' as well as 'contemplation' and 'invocation'. *Dhikr* is closely related to the 'prayer of the heart' of the Hesychasts of Eastern Christianity.

The goal of the mystical path is the transcending of the ego, and this path cannot be embarked upon without grace (*tawfiq*).[4]

Mention of *ar-Rūḥ* calls for the following remarks. In traditional metaphysics 'intellectual' or 'spiritual' are the adjectives pertaining to the third element in the ternary constituting the human being which, in scholastic terms, is: *corpus* (body), *anima* (soul), and *Spiritus vel Intellectus* (Spirit or Intellect). The middle term 'soul' comprises, amongst other things, the mind or reason, the adjectives pertaining to which are, of course, 'mental' or 'rational'. In slipshod modern parlance, however, the term 'intellectual' is often wrongly used as a synonym for these, in spite of the fact that it properly pertains only to 'Intellect' (or 'Spirit'). 'Intellectual' and 'spiritual' are more or less equivalent terms, the first putting the emphasis on the 'doctrinal' aspect and the second on the 'methodic' or 'realizational' aspect. Whereas body and soul are purely human and belong to the 'individual' domain, the

[4] *Fez, City of Islam*, Islamic Texts Society, Cambridge, England, in preparation.

Spirit or Intellect is 'universal' and transcends the human state as such. As already indicated, the Latin *Spiritus vel Intellectus* ('Spirit' or 'Intellect') corresponds to the Arabic *Rūḥ*. *Anima* ('soul') corresponds to the Arabic *nafs*.[5]

In Christianity, doctrines analogous to those of Sufism are to be found, in the Western Church, in the writings of Meister Eckhart, Angelus Silesius and certain others, and, in the Eastern Church, in the great exponents of apophatic and antinomian theology such as St Gregory Palamas, whose doctrine of the Divine Essence and the Divine Energies corresponds closely to the Sufi doctrine regarding *Dhāt* ('Essence') and *Ṣifāt* ('Qualities').

An essential difference between the two religions, however, is that whereas Islam possesses an exoteric domain—*shaī'a* or (outward) Law—and an esoteric domain—*ḥaqīqa* or (inward) Truth—no such division exists in Christianity. According to a certain Islamic point of view, Christianity is a pure *ḥaqīqa* (esoterism), which came into the world without a complementary exoteric component of its own. This view receives confirmation in Christ's own words: *regnum meum non est de hoc mundo.* Seen from this angle, certain ambiguities discernible in Christianity derive from the fact that, historically, this esoterism had to undergo an exoteric application, in an effort, so to speak, to make good the missing exoterism. This *de facto* extension of the Christian revelation (a *ḥaqīqa*, in Islamic terminology) to the outward domain could not, of course, in any way alter the original nature of the Chris-

[5] The nature and function of the Intellect are succinctly evoked in the words of Dante:

Io veggio ben che giammai non si sazia
nostro intelletto, se il ver non lo illustra.

Now do I see that never can our Intellect be sated,
unless that Truth do shine upon it.

tian dogmas and sacraments, which continue to be 'esoteric' formulations and 'initiatic' rites respectively.[6]

As far as the spiritualities of the two religions are concerned, Christian mysticism tends by and large to be characterized by the 'Way of Love' (*maḥabba*, in Islamic terminology),[7] whereas Islamic mysticism (i.e. Sufism) comprises both the 'Way of Knowledge' (*ma'rifa*) and the 'Way of Love' (*maḥabba*).[8] This is one reason why the more 'gnostic' or 'jñanic' formulations of Islamic mysticism tend to strike a foreign note to those familiar only with the Christian forms of spirituality.[9]

This distinction between Christianity and Islam (between 'Love' and 'Knowledge') also shows itself in the answers given by the two religions to the question: why was the world created? In Christianity it is customary to say that God created the world 'out of love'. While this statement would not be regarded as untrue in Islam either, a haunting and beautiful reference (more characteristic of the Islamic perspective) to the mystery of existence, is provided in the *ḥadīth qudsī*: 'I was a hidden treasure, and I wished to be *known*, so I created the world.'

*

* *

[6] See *Mystères Christiques* by Frithjof Schuon in *Etudes Traditionnelles*. Paris, July-August 1948.

[7] Some of those who, exceptionally, represent the 'Way of Knowledge' in Christianity, have just been mentioned.

[8] *Ma'rifa* and *maḥabba* correspond respectively to the *jñana-marga* and the *bhaktimarga* of the Hindus.

[9] It is also interesting to note in this connection that it is the very existence, in Islam, of an exoterism in the full sense of the word, that occasionally causes Christians to see something 'earthy' (not 'worldly'!) in some of the outward manifestations of Islam. Contrariwise, the exclusively esoteric nature of the Christian revelation tempts Muslims to regard Christians (who by and large fail to live up to the high spiritual demands of their 'esoterism') as hypocrites!

The doctrine of the 'oneness of being' has led some to believe that Sufi doctrine is a form of 'pantheism'. This is entirely misleading, as the term pantheism is normally used to designate certain European philosophic concepts of recent centuries that have nothing to do with any traditional doctrines, whether scholastic or mystical. Pantheism (the belief, for example, that God is the sum total of all things) implies a 'substantial' identity between the Principle and manifestation, or between the Creator and the created. This is foreign to all 'traditional' doctrine, which insists on the gulf between the Absolute and the relative, or the Infinite and the finite, going so far as to call the first element in each case 'Real' and the second (relatively) 'unreal'—because ephemeral.[10]

There is, however, an 'essential' (not 'substantial') identity between the created and the Creator, whence, precisely, the 'relative' reality of the world in which we live. Once again Sufi doctrine derives from the *shahāda*: 'there is no reality except Reality'. Here the reference is to the essential identity of all that is, and to the nothingness of that which is not. The Sufi doctrine of *waḥdat al-wujūd* is, in fact, the equivalent of the Vedantic *advaita*, which some have called 'monism', but which is perhaps more accurately translated as 'non-duality'.

The point is that the world does not have a different principle from God. As the Hindus have put it, 'the world *is* God (i.e. as far as its essential principle is concerned), but God is not the world'. This second proposition is, in fact, the basic error of latter-day European

[10] Cf. the saying of Christ: 'Heaven and earth shall pass away, but my words will not pass away.'

pantheistic trends, be these poetic or philosophic. Sufism, on the contrary, is an expression of traditional doctrine on this matter.

*

* *

It might be asked: what is Sufism's attitude towards the modern world and the belief in 'progress'? It is known that the Hindus teach that we are living in the latter period of the 'Dark Age' *(kali-yuga)*, in which men turn from the 'total' to the fragmentary, from the profound to the superficial, and from the spiritual to the material – at an ever-increasing pace, moreover, until mankind reaches the final, cataclysmic end. Similar doctrines and prophecies are to be found in Buddhism, Christianity and the religion of the North American Indians.

The Islamic view is given tersely in a Tradition *(ḥadīth)* of the Prophet: 'No time cometh upon you but is followed by a worse!' This sets the tone for the characteristic 'conservatism' of Sufism which, as far as the outward world is concerned, seeks above all to protect sacred – and salvific – forms from the erosions of time and ever-increasing indifference. Those living in the latter times enjoy certain compensations, however. In the Christian parable of the labourers in the vineyard, those who worked only for the last period before 'sunset', received the same wage as those who had worked throughout the whole day. And the Prophet of Islam declared that in the earliest days he who omitted a tenth of the Law would be damned, whereas in the latter days he who accomplishes a tenth of the Law will be saved. In the 'Dark Age' there can be no greater message of hope and encouragement for exoterist and esoterist alike.

*

* *

In the Introduction reference was made to the symbolism of the radii of a circle: the nearer they are to the centre, the nearer they are to each other, and in the centre itself the radii unite. It is naturally the esoteric doctrines – the doctrines of 'love' and 'gnosis' (or 'knowledge') – of the various religions that are closest to one another. If one compares social customs and laws of inheritance, one need not expect to find identity; but the nearer one gets to the 'centre' – to the doctrines concerning the glory of God, the indigence of man, the ways of salvation – the nearer one gets to unanimity. In India, the 'social' differences between Islam and Hinduism could scarcely be greater, yet Prince Dara Shikoh, son of the Emperor Shah Jahan and Mumtaz Mahal, declared: 'The science of Vedanta and the science of Sufism are one.'[11]

There is surely no more beautiful testimony to the transcendent unity of the religions than the haunting declaration of one of the great Islamic masters of 'gnosis', ash-Shaikh al-Akbar Muḥyi 'd-Dīn ibn 'Arabī, who flourished in Andalusia at the end of the twelfth and beginning of the thirteenth century: 'My heart has opened unto every form: it is a pasture for gazelles, a cloister for Christian monks, a temple for idols, the Ka'ba of the pilgrim, the tables of the Torah and the book of the Qur'ān. I practise the religion of Love; in

[11] Sikhism, for its part, seems to have resulted from a sort of fusion of Hindu *bhakti* and Muslim *maḥabba*.

whatsoever directions its caravans advance, the religion of Love shall be my religion and my faith.'[12]

Photo: Jean-Louis Michon

3. Tomb of Muḥyi 'd-Dīn ibn 'Arabī, near Damascus

[12] Regarding ibn 'Arabī's use of the expression 'the religion of Love', Frithjof Schuon comments as follows: 'Here it is not a question of *maḥabba* in the psychological or methodological sense, but of a truth that is lived, and of divine "attraction". Here "love" is opposed to "forms", which are envisaged as "cold" and "dead". St Paul also says that "the letter killeth, but the spirit maketh alive". "Spirit" and "love" are here synonymous.' (*Understanding Islam*, p. 42, Allen & Unwin, London, 1963, and Penguin Books, Baltimore, Maryland, 1972).

CHAPTER THREE

THE MYSTICAL PATH

All religion has as its object salvation, whatever degree or mode of the latter be envisaged. Religion is always doctrine with a view to 'realization'. The doctrine is never mere theory, but always 'operative' in intent. Consequently, in religion, doctrine and method, or theory and practice, are indissolubly wed. Doctrine concerns the mind (or, at the highest level, the 'intellect' in the Medieval and Sufi sense of this term); method (or practice) concerns the will. Religion, to be itself, must always engage both 'mind' and 'will'.

The 'operative' side of religion, in the ordinary sense of this term, manifests itself in two main ways: morality and worship. Morality is self-explanatory: 'doing the things which ought to be done and not doing the things which ought not to be done'; worship takes two forms: participation in the public rites of the religion, and the performance of private works of piety, classically summed up under the headings 'prayer' and 'fasting'.[1]

Religion, then, is concerned with salvation. In order to embark on the path that leads to salvation one must obviously be a member of the religion which teaches it and which, on certain conditions, 'guarantees' it. Salvation is ordinarily conceived as being attainable

[1] This is a general (and not a specifically Islamic) reference to privāte devotions. It is not a reference to the public Islamic rites of *ṣalāt* and *ramaḍān*.

only after death – a rejoining of the saints in paradise. The only difference between spirituality (or mysticism) and religion in the ordinary sense, is that spirituality envisages as its main end the attaining of sanctity (or the embarking on the path that leads to sanctity) even in this life, here and now. All spiritual doctrine, and all spiritual method, are orientated towards this end. This is what the mystical or initiatic path is all about.

To embark on a spiritual path, a rite of initiation is indispensable. This is the case in all of the religions. The rite of initiation, which may be compared to the planting of a seed, imparts on the disciple a specific spiritual influence which effectuates the beginning (*initium*) of his 'new', inward, life. No seed, no life, no growth. No initiation, no rebirth, no sanctification. In Sufism, the aspirant receives the rite of initiation from a Sufi master (*shaikh* or *murshid*) who, in his turn, has received it, at the beginning of his spiritual career, from his *shaikh* or spiritual master, and so on back to the Prophet himself who, by Divine Grace, initiated the first Sufis.

The name 'Sufi' did not exist in the time of the Prophet, but the reality did. The Prophet conferred this rite (and gave the corresponding counsels) to only some of his Companions; they in turn passed it on, and in this way, up to the present day, the rite, in unbroken succession, is still passed on. This chain of initiation is known in Arabic as *silsila*. The various Sufi methods of spiritual realization (to which reference will later be made) cannot validly be practised without the initiation, and the counsel, of a *shaikh* or spiritual master. To attempt to do so would be to court considerable spiritual danger.

The majority of Muslims are not Sufis, and have not received this rite of initiation. The situation in Christianity is rather different. The Christian rite of initiation is baptism. It is clear that since early times baptism has been routinely administered to infants. In this, Christianity is exceptional, for it is unusual for initiation to be conferred on all, and also at an age which rules out conscious desire on the part of those to be initiated. This state of affairs, however, springs from the historical phenomenon in Christianity earlier referred to, namely the application of an esoterism *(ḥaqīqa)* to the exoteric or social domain, thus causing it to play a role analogous to that of the *sharīʿa* in Islam.

Nevertheless, since an esoteric rite applied exoterically remains esoteric in itself, it follows that all Christians are in principle initiates; that is, their spiritual status is in principle analogous to that of the Sufis.[2] Certainly a Christian seeking to embark on a spiritual path within Christianity has no need of further initiation. The overwhelming majority of Christians, of course, do not seek to exploit in any full sense the initiation which they indubitably possess. Technically (if not actually) speaking, they are comparable to those Muslims (*mutabarrikūn*)[3] who receive the rite of initiation, not with the intention of following a spiritual path, but for the sake of its 'blessing' (*baraka*) and as a reinforcement of their pious efforts faithfully to observe the law of Islam. Christian initiation (baptism) is exploited fully only by the saints. Frithjof Schuon

[2] It will be recalled that, although, strictly speaking, the term *Ṣūfī* applies only to those who have reached the goal (the saints), it is permissible also to apply it, by extension, to all who have received initiation with a view to travelling along the path.

[3] Cf. *sālikūn*, 'travellers' along the spiritual path.

has referred to the difference between Islam and Christianity in this domain as follows: 'In Islam there is no sanctity other than in esoterism; in Christianity there is no esoterism other than in sanctity.'

In Sufism, the aspirant must fulfil two general conditions or requirements in order to be accepted. These are fervent adherence to the faith and law of Islam (the *sharī'a)* and the practice of (or a sincere and whole-hearted desire to practise) the virtues.

*

* *

An indispensable element in Sufi organization is the spiritual master or *shaikh*, around whom disciples gather and from whom disciples receive the initiation which, through a long chain (*silsila*), is ultimately derived from the Prophet himself. Many generations having occurred between the time of the Prophet and the present day, the *silsilas* are now many and complex, but all of them can be traced back to one or other of those Companions whom the Prophet himself initiated, notably to the Caliphs Abu Bakr and 'Alī. An excellent example of these 'chains of descent' is provided by Martin Lings in his book *A Sufi Saint of the Twentieth Century.*[4] The 'family tree' of Sufi masters, from the earliest times to the present day, is replete with examples of outstanding holiness. In many instances the names of these saints have been given to those 'branches' of the tree over which their particular radiance shines. These branches (Sufi 'orders' or 'brotherhoods') are known as *ṭuruq* (singular *ṭarīqa*='path'), and are indeed so many paths to

[4] Allen & Unwin, London, 1971. pp. 232–3.

ḥaqīqa, the Inward, Divine Reality, or, in other words, to God Himself.

The first great Sufi order to appear in the form in which *ṭuruq* are now known was the Qādirī *ṭarīqa*, which took its name from its illustrious founder, the Shaikh 'Abd al-Qādir al-Jilānī (1078–1166). This was an offshoot of the older Junaidī *ṭarīqa* which stemmed from the great Abu 'l-Qāsim al-Junaid of Baghdad (d. 910). Amongst the next to appear were the Suhrawardī *ṭarīqa*, whose founder was Shihāb ad-Dīn as-Suhrawardī (1144-1234), and the venerable Shādhilī *ṭarīqa*, founded by one of the greatest luminaries of Western Islam, the Shaikh Abū 'l-Ḥasan ash-Shādhilī (1196–1258). Another order to be created about the same period was the Maulawī *ṭarīqa* (more famous under its Turkish name Mevlevi), so called after the title *Maulānā* ('our Lord'), given by his disciples to the founder of the order, Jalāl ad-Dīn Rūmī (1207–73), author of the *Mathnawī*, and perhaps the greatest mystical poet of Islam. The most characteristic feature of the Mevlevi order is the famous whirling dance performed by the *fuqarā*[5] as an outward support for their *dhikr* ('invocation' or 'quintessential prayer'). This dance is still performed at Konya in Turkey where Rūmī's tomb is located.[6]

In spite of all the differences between them, one cannot refrain from comparing these four venerable Sufi orders (which crystallized in the twelfth and thirteenth centuries and which exist down to the present day) with the three great monastic orders of Western Christendom (which were likewise formed in the Middle Ages, and

[5] Plural of *faqīr* (poor, 'poor in spirit'). Members of Sufi orders are known as *fuqarā* (or, in the Persian form, 'dervishes'). This is how Sufis refer to themselves.

[6] See *Sufism* by A. J. Arberry (Allen & Unwin, 4th imp., 1972).

4. 'Indication of the Brotherhoods' *(bayān aṭ-ṭuruq)*
(These words are inscribed on the crescent.)

At the foot of the trunk is the name *Allāh*. Above this are the names Gabriel and Muḥammad. The four large leaves at the top of the trunk bear the names of the first four Caliphs. The names of the different brotherhoods *(ṭuruq)* are inscribed

took their names from their founding saints) Benedictines, Dominicans and Franciscans. Having made the comparison, let one distinguishing mark immediately be mentioned: the Sufi orders do not impose celibacy, though their members may well be committed to exacting fasts, abstinences and vigils.[7]

The most renowned Sufi order to originate in India – and which did so at about the same time as those mentioned above – is the Chishti *ṭarīqa*, founded by Mu'īn ad-Dīn Chishti (1142–1236), whose tomb at Ajmer is one of the greatest shrines in the sub-continent,

[7] Mention of the differences between monks and *fuqarā* recalls the friendship, a generation ago, between the Bishop of Tripoli (a Franciscan of humble origin) and the Mayor (a muslim of noble lineage). The Mayor was rich, married, and a leader of men, yet so much did his piety shine through the existential 'envelopes' surrounding it, that the Bishop declared that in few other people had he seen the three monastic vows of poverty, chastity and obedience exemplified to such a high degree. This judgement may strike some as strange, but what the perceptive Bishop had detected was that the Mayor possessed 'detachment', and detachment from riches is 'poverty', detachment in marriage is 'chastity' and detachment when exercising authority is 'obedience' to the Source of all authority. Thus outward differences between Sufis and monks do not necessarily preclude that inwardly their essential qualities may be the same. See *A Cure for Serpents* by the Duke Alberto Denti di Pirajno (Pan Books, London, 1957, pp. 151–60).

---

on the leaves of the tree, but not in any particular order. As explained on pp. 56–61, each brotherhood is named after its founding saint, through whom, by a chain (*silsila*) of previous saints, it can trace its spiritual descent back either to 'Alī or Abu Bakr, and thence to the Prophet.

On the five-pointed star (symbol of the Five Pillars of Islam) are the words 'The Book [of God] and the Wont [of the Prophet]'. (*Al-Kitāb wa 's-Sunna*). For the symbolism of the crescent, see *The Book of Certainty* by Abu Bakr Sirāj ad-Dīn (Rider, London, 1952, and Samuel Weiser, New York, 1971), p. 23.

and is much visited and revered by Hindus and Muslims alike. Another order important throughout the East is the Naqshbandī order, founded in the fourteenth century by Pīr Muḥammad Naqshbandī. A widely disseminated order in Western Islam is the Darqāwī, a relatively recent sub-group of the Shādhilī *ṭarīqa*, having been founded by the Moroccan *shaikh* Mulay al-'Arabī

© *The International Rumi Society* *Photo: Dr James Dickie*

5. *Majlis* and *dhikr* of the Mevlevi dervishes (from a nineteenth-century woodcut)

ad-Darqāwī (c. 1743–1823). An illustrious spiritual descendant of Mulay al-'Arabī ad-Darqāwī was the Algerian *shaikh* Aḥmad al-'Alawī (1869–1934), 'whose erudition and saintliness', as A. J. Arberry has written, 'recall the golden age of the medieval mystics'.[8]

It should be mentioned that the founding of an order or brotherhood by an outstanding *shaikh* does not in any

[8] *Luzac's Oriental List*, London, October–December 1961.

way mean the creation of a new 'sect'. All the Sufi orders are expressions of Islamic spirituality, and are only differentiated in that each one is 'perfumed' by the *baraka* ('blessing') of its original founder, and employs the spiritual methods taught by that particular master. The 'whirling' of the Mevlevis and the spiritual retreat *(khalwa)* of the Darqāwīs are examples of particular methods pertaining to a given order.

*

* *

The practice of the religion of Islam involves the believer in the three great categories *islām* ((submission to the revealed law), *īmān* (faith in the *shahāda*) and *iḥsan* (virtue or sincerity). The following Tradition *(ḥadīth)* was reported by the Caliph 'Umar:

> One day when we were with the Messenger of God there came unto us a man whose clothes were of exceeding whiteness and whose hair was of exceeding blackness, nor were there any signs of travel upon him, although none of us had seen him before. He sat down knee unto knee opposite the Prophet, upon whose thighs he placed the palms of his hands, saying: 'O Muḥammad, tell me what is the surrender unto God (*al-islām*).' The Prophet answered: 'The surrender is that thou shouldst perform the prayer, bestow the alms, fast Ramaḍān, and make, if thou canst, the pilgrimage to the Holy House.' He said: 'Thou hast spoken truly' and we were amazed that having questioned him he should corroborate him. Then he said: 'Tell me what is faith (*īmān*)', and the Prophet answered: 'It is that thou shouldst believe in God and His Angels and His Books and His Apostles and the Last Day, and thou shouldst believe that no good or evil cometh but by His Providence.' 'Thou hast spoken truly', he said, and then: 'Tell me what is excellence *(iḥsan)*.' The Prophet

> answered: 'It is that thou shouldst worship God as if thou sawest Him, for if thou seest Him not, verily He seeth thee'... Then the stranger went away, and I stayed there long after he had gone, until the Prophet said to me: 'O 'Umar, knowest thou the questioner, who he was?' I said: 'God and His Prophet know best, but I know not at all.' 'It was Gabriel' said the Prophet. 'He came to teach you your religion.'[9]

The following of a spiritual way (the 'operative' side of Sufism) implies the inner illumination of *islām* and *īmān* by *iḥsān*. It necessitates a true vocation, and dedication of a heroic order. The central spiritual method of Sufism, as we shall see presently, is *dhikr* ('invocation'), but before aspiring to make use of this, the Sufi must first have a symbolic understanding of the Five Pillars of Islam (faith, prayer, fasting, almsgiving, pilgrimage) and practise them in an 'inward' manner. This is indeed an aspect of the Way itself. The Sufi interpretation of faith (*īmān*) has been indicated in the last chapter. As for ritual prayer (*ṣalāt*), the Sufi sees this, not only as an expression of man's 'slavehood' (*'ubūdiya*) towards his Lord (*Rabb*), but also as the creature's participation in the song of praise that binds the whole of creation to the Creator. *Ṣalāt* is performed not only by ordinary men, but also by prophets and even angels, and leads them into the invisible channels along which flow the blessings (*ṣalāt*) and the peace (*salām*) of God. Fasting (*ṣawm*) is a reminder of the utter dependence of the 'poor' (*fuqarā*) on Him Who is 'rich beyond any need of all the worlds' (*ghāniyun 'āni 'l-'ālamīn*). Almsgiving (*zakāt*) reminds the Sufi of his initiatic vow that all his

[9] Translated by Martin Lings. See *A Sufi Saint of the Twentieth Century* (Allen & Unwin, London, 1971), p. 44.

goods and his very life belong only to God, and also that he and his brothers are 'members one of another'. Finally the pigrimage (*ḥajj*) to the Ka'ba in Mecca is the outward symbol of the inward journey to the 'heart' (*qalb*), which is the seat of the Intellect (*'aql*) and is the mysterious centre where the Divine Spirit (*ar-Rūḥ*) touches the human soul.

*

*   *

Another important Sufi practice which is, so to speak, preparatory for the *dhikr* (the invocatory prayer which vehicles the Sufi's 'remembrance' of God) is the recitation of the *wird* or rosary. The *wird* differs slightly from one *ṭarīqa* to another, but it always comprises essentially the same three formulas. In the first, the *faqīr* asks forgiveness of God. In the second, he asks God to bless the Prophet and give him Peace. The third formula comprises the *shahāda*, the attestation of the Divine Unity. The *wird* is normally recited morning and evening, each formula being repeated a hundred times, for which purpose a chaplet (*subḥa* or *tasbīḥ*) is used.

The first formula symbolically represents the Sufi's 'movement' from outward to inward, from 'existence' to 'Being', from the human to the Divine. The second formula is the Sufi's participation in the Muhammadan Norm (which is permeated and sustained, precisely, by the Divine Blessing [*ṣalāt*] and Peace [*salām*]). It is a symbolic re-integration of the 'fragment' (man) in the Totality (Muḥammad), Muḥammad being the personification of the total Creation. The Muhammadan Norm is referred to by some Sufis as *al-insān al-kāmil*, 'Universal Man'. The third formula ('there is no reality other than the Reality') represents the extinction of everything that is not God. The Qur'ān *says: 'All on the earth shall pass away (fān)*; there remaineth (*yabqā*) but the face of thy Lord resplendent with Majesty and Bounty' (*Sura of the All-Merciful*, 26–27).[10] From the foregoing it can be seen that the three formulas of the *wird* correspond to the three 'stages'

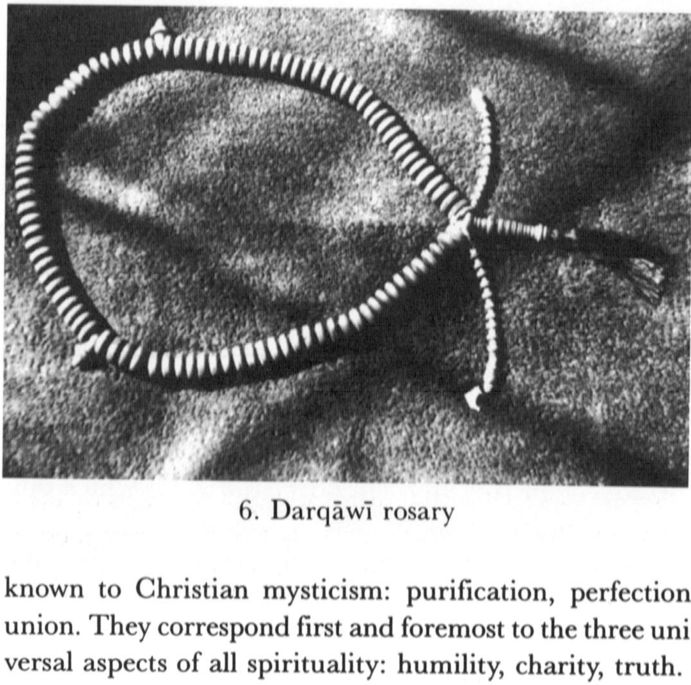

6. Darqāwī rosary

known to Christian mysticism: purification, perfection, union. They correspond first and foremost to the three universal aspects of all spirituality: humility, charity, truth.

*

*   *

[10] This verse is the origin of the Sufi concepts of 'extinction' (*fanā*) and 'Subsistence' (*baqā*). The 'extinction of extinction' (*fana' al-fanā*) spoken of by some Sufis corresponds to 'Subsistence' (*baqā*). For a Christian parallel, see footnote p. 49.

The Sufi spiritual method *par excellence* is the *dhikr*. This word, often translated as 'invocation', has the dual meaning of 'remembrance' and 'mention'. The Qur'ān is replete with injunctions to 'remember' God by invoking His Name: 'Invoke the Name of thy Lord and devote thyself to Him with utter devotion' (*Sura of the Enshrouded One*, 8). 'Remember God with much remembrance' (*Sura of the Confederates*, 41). 'Ritual prayer (*ṣalāt*) preserves from uncleanness and grave sin, but verily the remembrance of God is greater (*wa la dhikru 'Llāhi akbar*)' (*Sura of the Spider*, 45). 'Verily in the remembrance of God do hearts find rest' (*Sura of the Thunder*, 28). 'Remember Me and I shall remember you' (*Sura of the Cow*, 152).

Man finds himself entrapped in manifestation. Manifestation is doomed to impermanence, and this impermanence inevitably entails separation, suffering and death. All traditional metaphysics teaches that the Principle alone is permanent – and blissful. Once again we are brought back to the message of the *shahāda*: 'there is no permanence except in the Permanent', 'there is no reality other than the Real'. The doctrine of the *dhikr* is that the Divine Name (*Allāh*) directly vehicles the Principle, and when the believer unites himself with the Divine Name in fervent invocation, he inwardly frees himself from manifestation and its concomitant suffering.

Virtual at first, this liberation becomes effective through perseverance and the grace of God *tawfīq*). Without the grace of God, the *dhikr* can be a mortal danger. Hence the prohibition to attempt to practise it 'methodically' without initiation and the guidance of a *shaikh*. Any Muslim, however, provided his intention is just, may practise the *dhikr* intermittently and for short periods. In Sufism, on the other hand, the *dhikr* is central to the spiritual method and, in principle, the Sufi seeks to practise it, under the guidance of a spiritual master, without interruption. The two main supports for the *dhikr* are the *majlis* (session, meeting or gathering of *fuqarā*) and the *khalwa* (spiritual retreat). In most *ṭuruq*, *majālis* (plural of *majlis*) are held at regular intervals under the aegis of the *shaikh* or his representative (*muqaddam*), and at them the *fuqarā* may make the *dhikr* together for an hour or two. This may be done silently or in the form of a chant, motionlessly or accompanied by a rhythmic swaying which may take the form of a dance.

Sometimes the *dhikr* (and the dance, when present) is accompanied by the rhythmic beating of a drum or by music, either vocal or instrumental. *Khalawāt* (plural of *khalwa*) are solitary spiritual retreats for the purpose of invocation. These are made from time to time and may last for as short as several hours or as long as several days. Complementary to these two 'formal' supports for the *dhikr* is the frequent (in principle constant) silent invocation of the Divine Name at all times of the day, in the midst of other activities.

The symbolism of alchemy is sometimes used to describe the practice of the *dhikr*. The soul in its chaotic, unregenerate state is 'lead'. The philosopher's stone is the Divine Name, in contact with which the 'leaden' soul is transmuted into 'gold', which is its true nature. This true nature has been lost, but is recovered by the practice of the *dhikr*. The 'alchemical work' thus symbolizes the 'work of spiritual realization'. In either case the essential operation is a 'transmutation' of that which is 'base' into that which is 'noble'. The science of the macrocosm (the outward world) thus analogically coincides with the science of the microcosm (the inward world, or soul).

The Sufi doctrine of the *dhikr* coincides with that taught by the nineteenth-century Hindu saint Ramakrishna, who succinctly summed it up in the phrase: 'God and His Name are one.' In Hinduism the method of constant invocation of the Divine Name (or of a formula, *mantra*, containing a Divine Name) is known as *japa*. The Psalms, Gospels and the Epistles of St Paul are full of allusions to the saving power of God's Name: 'Whoever calls on the Name of the Lord shall be saved.' In Eastern Christianity, invocation of the Divine Name (the 'prayer without ceasing' enjoined by St Paul) takes the form of the 'Jesus Prayer', a practice made familiar by the widely disseminated *Way of a Pilgrim*. In Western Christendom, the revelations made to Sister Consolata, an Italian Capuchin nun, in the earlier part of this century, revived the Medieval invocation *Jesu-Maria*.[11] Thus do the religions meet, not only in pure metaphysics, but also in pure prayer.

That 'God and His Name are one' is beautifully brought out by the Arabic language, by virtue of the multiple forms that can be assumed by the basic triliteral root. Thus from *dha-ka-ra*, to invoke or remember, are derived *Madhkūr* (the Invoked), *Dhākir* (the Invoker) and *Dhikr* (Invocation). In the last analysis, according to Sufi doctrine, it is God Himself who invokes, God Himself who is invoked, and God Himself who is the invocation. That this divine Act should pass through man is the mystery of salvation.

Metaphysically speaking, *Madhkūr-Dhākir-Dhikr*

[11] One of the greatest Catholic practitioners of the Holy Name in post-medieval times was St Bernardine of Siena (fifteenth century).

corresponds to the Hindu ternary *Sat-Chit-Ananda*. *Sat* is the Divine Object, *Chit* is the Divine Subject and *Ananda* is Divine Union. *Sat-Chit-Ananda*, often translated as 'Being-Consciousness-Bliss' (hence 'Object-Subject-Union'), also corresponds to the Christian Trinity 'Father – Son – Holy Spirit'. This is all the more apparent when one recalls St Augustine's designation of the Trinity as 'Being-Wisdom-Life'.[12]

The practice of the *dhikr* goes hand-in-hand with the practice of the virtues. Virtue is seen essentially as self-effacement (*faqr* or poverty) and it is said that there can be no *dhikr* without *faqr*. Once again the Arabic language makes apparent an essential identity of content when the same truth is given a different form: only the *faqīr* (the one who is 'poor in spirit') may be a *dhākir* (one who invokes God).

The Qur'ān forges the link between *dhikr* and virtue, when it says: 'Call upon your Lord humbly and in secret. Lo, He loveth not transgressors. Work not confusion in the earth after the fair ordering thereof, and call on Him in fear and hope. Verily the mercy of God is nigh unto the good.' (*Sura of the Heights*, 55–56).

The virtues tend to fall into two groups: the active virtues and the passive ones. Frithjof Schuon has explained how spiritual 'activity' and spiritual 'passivity' have their prototypes in two Quranic passages (one about the palm-tree and the other about the *miḥrāb* or prayer niche) concerning the Virgin Mary (Sayyidatnā Maryam).[13] The Qur'ān, incidentally, contains more references to the Virgin Mary than do the Gospels,

[12] *Sat-Chit-Ananda* may also be interpreted as 'Known-Knower-Knowledge' or 'Beloved-Lover-Love'.

[13] *Dimensions of Islam* (Allen & Unwin, London, 1970) pp. 90–93.

and some Sufis see in her the personification of all virtues. The first passage, relating to the Nativity of Christ, is as follows:

> And make mention, in the Book, of Mary, when she withdrew from her people to a chamber (in the Temple) facing east, and chose seclusion from them. And We sent unto her Our Spirit (Gabriel), and he took before her the form of a perfect man. And she said: 'I take refuge from thee in the All-Merciful. If thou art God-fearing.' He said: 'I am but a messenger of thy Lord, that I may bestow on thee a holy son.' She said: 'How can I have a son when no mortal hath touched me, neither have I been unchaste?' He said: 'So it shall be. Thy Lord hath said: "Easy is this for Me. And We will make of him a sign for mankind and a mercy from Us. It is a thing decreed."' And she conceived him, and retired with him to a far-off place. And the throes came upon her by the trunk of the palm-tree. She said: 'Would that I had died ere this, and become a thing forgotten!' Then one cried unto her from below her: 'Grieve not! Thy Lord hath placed a rivulet beneath thee, and shake the trunk of the palm-tree toward thee, thou wilt cause ripe dates to fall upon thee. So eat and drink and be consoled.' (*Sura of Mary,* 16-26)

The second passage is the following:

> Whenever Zachariah went into the sanctuary (*miḥrāb*) where she was, he found her supplied with food. 'O Mary,' he said, 'whence hast thou this?' She said, 'It is from God. Verily God supplieth whom He will without reckoning.' (*Sura of the Family of* 'Imrān, 37).

In this interpretation, the 'shaking' of the palm-tree refers to the 'active' virtues and above all to *dhikr*. 'Withdrawal into the *miḥrāb*' symbolizes self-effacement or *faqr*.

The Quranic references to Jesus are also numerous.

For the Qur'ān, Jesus is the Messiah, the incarnate Word of God (IV, 171), the son of Mary ever-Virgin (XXI, 91), who was sent by God to confirm the Pentateuch with the Gospel, which is guidance and light (V, 49). Mary and her son have deserved the admiration of the Universe (XXI, 91). 'Every son of Adam, at birth is touched by Satan, save only the son of Mary and his Mother.' (*ḥadīth*) The Qur'ān makes specific mention of the resurrection of Christ (IV, 156–8; XIX, 33). As mentioned earlier, whereas Muḥammad is referred to as the 'Seal of Prophecy' (*khātim an-nubuwwa*), Christ is referred to by some Sufis as the 'Seal of Sanctity' (*khātim al-wilaya*). In his celebrated work *Al-Futūḥāt al-Makkiya* (' The Meccan Revelations') (II, 64–5), Muḥyi 'd-Dīn ibn 'Arabī comments on this as follows: 'The Seal of universal holiness, above which there is no other holy, is our Lord Jesus. We have met several contemplatives of the heart of Jesus. . . . I myself have been united to him several times in my ecstasies, and by his ministry I returned to God at my conversion. . . . He has given me the name of friend and has prescribed austerity and nakedness of spirit.'

*

* *

The highest state of mystical union or 'supreme identity' has been expressed in many different ways. Sometimes such expressions, when in subjective mode, are arrestingly direct. One thinks of St Paul's 'Not I, but Christ in me' and Al-Hallāj's 'I am the Truth' (*anā 'l-Ḥaqq*). In objective mode, there is the Hindu *Tat tvam asi* ('thou art That') and there is the Buddhist assertion that *samsara* (the relative) is *Nirvana* (the Absolute). (Not the opposite way round, of course, as has already been emphasized on pp. 49–50. The reference here is to the 'oneness of essence' between the creature and the Creator. In the medieval phrase: *Quis adhaeret Deo, unus spiritus est.*)

One of the expressions of the Supreme Identity found in Hinduism and Buddhism is that of *Tantra*, which makes use of the symbolism of sexual union (*maithuna*). This symbolism is often the subject of Hindu and Buddhist statuary. In the Hindu form,[14] it is basically a question of the union of Shiva (God) with His *Shakti* or Consort (representing his own creative 'Powers' or 'Energies', separated from Him, nonetheless, in so far as He is infinite and 'unqualified' [*nirguna*].[15] Shiva and his *Shakti* are the divine prototypes of *purusha* and *prakriti*, which can be translated into Western scholastic terms as Essence and Substance, or Act and Potency.

The first of these two terms represents the Active Pole, and the second the Passive Pole, of universal manifestation. Each of these Poles has 'dynamic' and 'static' modes. For example, in medieval terms, the dynamic mode of the Passive Pole is *Natura* and the static mode of the Passive Pole is *Materia*.[16] In *Tantra*, it is characteristically a question of the union between the static mode of the Active Pole and the dynamic mode of the Passive Pole. We are here on the threshold of the mystery of Creation itself. It is this creative process that is reflected in all traditional art. In the words of St

[14] In the Buddhist form, it is a question of the 'marriage of wisdom and method', *prajna* and *upaya*.

[15] This is reminiscent of the doctrine of St Gregory Palamas.

[16] The dynamic and static aspects of the Active Pole are respectively *Spiritus* and *Intellectus*. This exposition is taken from Titus Burckhardt's *Alchemy* (Robinson & Watkins, London, 1967, and Penguin Books, Baltimore, U.S.A., 1971), Chapter 9 'Nature can overcome Nature'.

Thomas Aquinas: 'Art is the imitation of Nature (*Natura*) in her mode of operation.' This is, precisely, the dynamic mode of the Passive Pole.

In *Tantra*, then, it is not merely a question of the union of Active and Passive, or dynamic and static. The unique strength of the bond comes precisely from the union of 'static' Activity with 'dynamic' Passivity. The intimacy of this union is reflected in many arts. It is particularly clear, for example, in the symbolism of weaving, where the warp and the weft stand in a 'sexual' relationship to one another. 'The weft' (dynamic, but nevertheless – because horizontal – passive and feminine) 'darts in and out of the warp' (static, but nevertheless – because vertical – active and masculine) 'like a streak of lightning or an arrow speeding to its mark; like a ship, it plies from shore to shore, out and home again; like Lakshmi casting flowers in Vishnu's lap, it adorns and nourishes its Lord'.[17]

The expression 'static Activity' recalls the Taoist concept of the 'actionless Act',[18] and indeed the doctrine of *Tantra* is well expressed in the Taoist symbol of *Yin-Yang*. The Active (or masculine) Pole, *Yang*, is represented by a white field, but his 'motionlessness' is represented by a black spot in the centre. The Passive (or feminine) Pole, *Yin*, is represented by a black field, but her 'dynamism' is represented by a white spot. The intimacy of their union and the strength of their bond are represented by the sinuous intertwining (reminiscent of a Tantric statue) of the two fields, in the well-known symbol:

[17] From 'A Craft as a Fountain of Grace and a Means of Realization' by Artistide Messinesi (in *Art and Thought*, Luzac, London, 1947, p. 38).

[18] Cf. the 'motionless Mover' of Aristotle.

Incidentally, a black field, taken by itself, and with the white spot in its centre, vividly recalls the Black Virgin of Christian iconography. One thinks, for example, of the celebrated Madonna (with the Child Jesus) at Czenstochowa in Poland. In Christian terms, spiritual realization has been described as the 'passage from Potency to Act'.

All these considerations have not taken us away from our main theme, namely, the mystical path, and spiritual realization, in Sufism.[19] The Active and Passive Poles, and their union, are central to Sufi doctrine and method. In Sufi writings, the Polarity in question appears as the Divine Command (*al-Amr*) and Universal Nature (*aṭ-Ṭabī' at al-kulliya*); and again as the Supreme Pen (*al-Qalam*) and the Guarded Tablet

[19] The numerous references to non-Islamic mysticisms in this book have been introduced, firstly, because all religions are now on our doorstep (or at least are known to scholarship) and it is thus natural to speak of them and make comparisons; and secondly, because expounding a particular principle in the terms of another religion can often throw light on the same principle as it occurs in the religion under study. The Prophet said: 'Seek ye wisdom, even if it be in China!'

(*al-Lawḥ al-maḥfūẓ*).[20] This relationship is at the heart of Islamic metaphysics, while in mysticism (as well as in art), use is made of the fact that the 'creating' pathway leading from Principle to manifestation is also the 're-integrating' pathway leading from manifestation to Principle.[21]

The application of the 'sexual' symbolism may sometimes be reversed, and there are some Sufis who attribute femininity, not to the Passive Pole of manifestation, but to the Divine Essence (*Dhāt*).[22] This has above all a 'mystical' or 'operative' end in view, the goal of the mystical quest being personified as a woman, usually named Laila which means 'night' (again a reference to the Divine Essence).[23] 'This is the holiest and most secret inwardness of God, and marks the end of the mystical path.'[24] In this symbolism Laila and *ḥaqīqa* (Divine Reality) are one. The Virgin Mary (Sayyidat-nā Maryam), who personifies not only all the virtues but also Divine Mercy (*Raḥma*), is identified by some Sufis with Laila.

It is not surprising that many Sufi poems take the

[20] See *Introduction to Sufi Doctrine* by Titus Burckhardt (Thorsons, 1976), Chapter V.

[21] The outward form of the 'incarnationist' Christian religion could scarcely be more different from that of Islam, centred as the latter is on the saving power of truth alone (the quintessence of this being the *Shahāda*). And yet the most direct Christian expression of the reality just referred to is one of the classic formulations (first enunciated by St Irenaeus) of the Christian doctrine of the Incarnation: 'God became man, so that man might become God.'

[22] In Arabic *Dhāt* (Essence) is feminine in gender.

[23] This 'subjective' attitude is not unrelated to the 'objective' doctrine of *Sat-Chit-Ananda* seen as 'Beloved-Lover-Love'. Likewise, in the Buddhist form of *Tantra* it is Wisdom (*prajna*) which is feminine, and Method (*upaya*) which is masculine.

[24] Martin Lings, 'Sufism', in *Man, Myth and Magic*, No. 97, p. 2713, London, 1972.

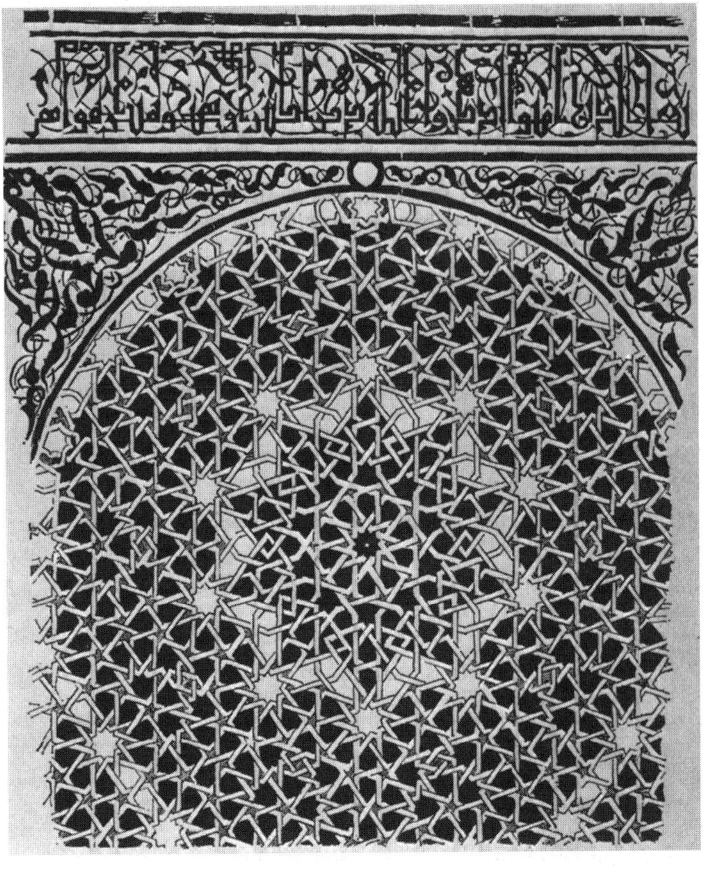

7. Typical Islamic geometrical design
(From the 'Attarīn Medersa, Fez.)

'The idea dominating all Islamic art is that of unity.
The world manifests Divine Unity in multiple mode.
"Unity in Multiplicity" mirrors "Multiplicity in Unity".'
Titus Burckhardt

form of love lyrics. The name Laila is also that of the heroine of the best-known love story of the Muslim world, Laila and Majnūn.

It goes without saying, of course, that in the 'ordinary' relationship between the human soul and God, the soul is passive and 'feminine', while God is active and 'masculine'. It is in the mystical path that the symbolic relationship may sometimes be reversed.

APPENDIX

Selection of quotations relating to Sufism

(a) **from the Qur'ān**

In the Name of God, the Clement, the Merciful,
Praise be to God, the Lord of the worlds,
The Clement, the Merciful,
The owner of the Day of Judgement,
Thee we worship and in Thee we seek refuge.
Guide us upon the straight path
The path of those to whom Thou art gracious,
Not of those upon whom Thine anger hath fallen,
Nor of those who are astray.
Amen.

The Opening Sura

He (God) is the First and the Last, the Outwardly Manifest and the Inwardly Hidden.

Sura of Iron, 3

Wheresoe'er ye turn, there is the Face of God.

Sura of the Cow, 115

We (God) are nearer to him (man) than his jugular vein.

Sura of Qaf, 16

God is the light of the Heavens and the earth.

Sura of Light, 35

All on the earth shall pass away; there abideth but the Face of thy Lord, resplendent with Majesty and Bounty.

Sura of the All-Merciful, 26-7

Men whom neither trade nor profit diverts from the remembrance of God.

Sura of Light, 37

Say: *Allāh*, and leave them to their idle prattle.

Sura of Cattle, 91

And bear with those who call on their Lord, morning and evening, seeking His Face.

Sura of the Cave, 28

And in the earth are portents for those whose faith is sure, and also in your souls. Can ye then not see?

Sura of the Winnowing Winds, 20-21

We shall show them Our signs on the horizons and in their souls, until it is clear to them that it is the Truth. Doth it not suffice as to thy Lord, that He is witness over everything?

Sura of the Expounded, 53

Verily we created the Heavens and the earth with naught but Truth, yet most men know not.

Sura of Smoke, 38-9

If my slaves ask thee of Me, say I am near. I answer the prayer of the pray-er when he prayeth.

Sura of the Cow, 186

God guides to His Light whom He pleases.

Sura of Light, 35

Verily God giveth beyond measure to whom He will.

Sura of the Family of 'Imrān, 37

And say: Truth hath come and falsehood hath vanished away. Verily falsehood is ever bound to vanish.

Sura of the Children of Israel, 81

And We have revealed the Qur'ān, which is a healing and a mercy for believers.

Sura of the Children of Israel, 82

And seek aid, through patience and prayer.

Sura of the Cow, 45

Fear God, for it is God Who teaches you.

Sura of the Cow, 282

They seek to extinguish God's light with their mouths, but though the unbelievers hate it, God will perfect His light. He it is who sent His Messenger with guidance and the religion of the Truth.

Sura of the Ranks, 8-9

There is no refuge from God but in Him.

Sura of Repentance, 118

Keep vigil all the night, save a little.

Sura of the Enshrouded One, 2

Glorify Him the livelong night.

Sura of Man, 26

Flee unto God.

Sura of the Winnowing Winds, 50

The seven heavens and the earth and all that is therein praise Him, and there is not a thing but hymneth His praise; but ye understand not their praise. Verily He is ever kind, forgiving.

Sura of the Children of Israel, 44

O men! Ye are the poor (*fuqarā*) in relation to God, and God is the Rich (*Ghanī*) to whom all praises are due.

Sura of the Creator, 15

It is not their eyes that are blind, but their hearts.

Sura of the Pilgrimage, 46

Verily we are God's and unto Him we shall return.

Sura of the Cow, 156

(b) **from the Traditions** (*aḥādīth*)

I was a hidden treasure, and I wished to be known, so I created the world.

ḥadīth qudsī

Verily My mercy taketh precedence over My wrath.

ḥadīth qudsī

Nothing is more pleasant to Me, as a means for My slave to draw nigh unto Me, than the worship that I have made binding upon him; and My slave ceaseth not to draw near unto Me by devotions of his free will until I love him; and when I love him, I am the hearing whereby he heareth and the sight whereby he seeth and the hand wherewith he smiteth and the foot whereon he walketh.

ḥadīth qudsī

My Heaven cannot contain Me, nor can My earth, but the heart of My believing slave can contain Me.

ḥadīth qudsī

God saith: Whoso doth one good act, for him are ten rewards: and I also give more to whomever I will; and whoso doth an ill, its punishment is equal to it, or I forgive him; and whoso seeketh to approach Me one span, I approach him one cubit; and whoso seeketh to approach Me one cubit, I approach him two fathoms; and whoso walketh towards Me, I run towards him; and whoso cometh before Me with an earth full of sins, and believeth solely in Me, him I come before with a face of forgiveness as big as the earth.

hadīth qudsī

God is beautiful, and He loves beauty.

All that is beautiful comes from the beauty of God.

Everything on earth is accursed, except the remembrance of God.

The heart of man is the Throne of God.

There is no strength and no power but in God.

No one shall meet *Allāh* who has not first met the Prophet.

He who has seen me (the Prophet), has seen the Truth (God).

Made worthy of love to me are perfumes and women, and there has been made a coolness for my eyes in prayer.

Our Lord – may He be blessed and exalted – comes down every night towards the earthly heavens at the time when there remains but the last third of the night, and He says: 'Who calls upon Me, that I may reply to Him? Who asks of Me something, that I may grant his request? Who asks of Me forgiveness, that I may forgive him?'

Whoso knoweth himself, knoweth his Lord.

Be in this world as a stranger or as a passer-by.

God hath ninety-nine Names; he that telleth them shall enter Paradise.

Whenever men gather together to invoke *Allāh*, they are surrounded by Angels, the Divine Favour envelops them, and Peace (*Sakīna*) descends upon them, and *Allāh* remembers them in His assembly.

There is a means of polishing all things whereby rust may be removed; that which polishes the heart is the invocation of *Allāh* and there is no act which removes the punishment of *Allāh* further from you than this invocation.

8. *Inna 'Llāha jamīlun, yuḥibbu 'l-jamāl*

'Verily God is beautiful and He loves beauty'

(Example of *Ṭhuluth* style of Arabic calligraphy)

Whoso protecteth God in his heart, him will God protect in the world.

The *sharī'a* is what I say (*aqwālī*), the *ṭarīqa* is what I do (*ā'amālī*) and the *ḥaqīqa* is what I am (*aḥwālī*).

(c) **from the Sufis**

My heart has opened unto every form: it is a pasture for gazelles, a cloister for Christian monks, a temple for idols, the Ka'ba of the pilgrim, the tables of the Torah and the book of the Qur'ān. I practise the religion of Love; in whatsoever directions its caravans advance, the religion of Love shall be my religion and my faith.

Muḥyi 'd-Dīn ibn 'Arabī (d. 1240)

Thine existence is a sin wherewith no other sin may be compared.

Rābi'a al-'Adawiya (d. 801)

My Lord, eyes are at rest, the stars are setting, hushed are the movements of the birds in their nests, of the monsters in the deep. And Thou art the Just who knoweth no change, the Equity that swerveth not, the Everlasting that passeth not away. The doors of kings are locked and guarded by their henchmen. But Thy door is open to whoso calleth on Thee. My Lord, each lover is now alone with his beloved. And I am alone with Thee.

Rābi'a al-'Adawiya (d. 801)

I and Thou signify duality, and duality is an illusion, for Unity alone is Truth (*al-Ḥaqq*, God). When the ego is gone, then God is His own mirror in me.

Abu Yazīd al-Bistāmī (d. 875)

The knowledge of God cannot be obtained by seeking, but only those who seek it find it.

Abu Yazīd al-Bistāmī (d. 875)

The end of knowledge is that man comes to the point where he was at the origin.

Abu Yazīd al-Bistāmī (d. 875)

I saw my Lord with the eye of the heart. I said: Who art Thou? He answered: Thou.

Mansūr al-Ḥallāj (d. 922)

O God, drown me in the essence of the Ocean of Divine Solitude, so that I neither see nor hear nor be conscious nor feel except through It.

'Abd as-Salām ibn Mashīsh (d. 1228)

No deed arising from a renouncing heart is small, and no deed arising from an avaricious heart is fruitful.

ibn 'Aṭā'illāh (d. 1309)

Everything outside of God is unreal, everything taken
individually or collectively, when you truly know it.
Know: without Him the whole creation, including you,
would disappear, and come to nothing.

Whatever does not have its root in His Being,
can in no wise be real.
The knowers of God are as if extinguished. What else can they look upon, but Him, the Transcendent, the Glorious?
Everything they see outside of Him, has truly been destined for destruction, in the past, in the future, and in the present moment...

Abu Madyan (d. 1197)

The Sufi sees his own existence as particles of dust made visible by a ray of sunlight: neither real nor unreal.

Abu'l-Ḥasan ash-Shādhilī (d. 1258)

Seekest thou Laila [Divine Reality], when she is manifest within thee? Thou deemest her to be other, but she is not other than thou.

Muḥammad al-Ḥarrāq (d. 1845)

The beauty of man is in his intelligence and the intelligence of woman is in her beauty.

Sufi saying

Truth melteth like snow in the hands of him whose soul melteth not like snow in the hands of Truth.

Sufi saying

FURTHER READING

A. Books on Sufism

Arberry, A. J. *Sufism:* Allen & Unwin, 4th imp. 1972.
Useful historical sketch, but with major blindspot regarding later Sufism.

Burckhardt, Titus. *Introduction to Sufi Doctrine*. Thorsons, 1976.
Masterly exposition of Islamic metaphysics.

———. *Moorish Culture in Spain:* Allen & Unwin, 1972.
Authoritative descriptions of every aspect of traditional Muslim civilization, with an excellent chapter on the Mystics. Beautifully illustrated.

———. *Fez, City of Islam*: Islamic Texts Society, Cambridge, England, in preparation.
Perhaps the best general introduction available to Islamic civilization, piety, philosophy, and art.

Lings, Martin. 'Sufism'. In *Religion in the Middle East*, edited by A. J. Arberry, vol. 2, chap. 13, pp. 253–69. Cambridge University Press, 1969.
A splendid and moving account.

———. *A Sufi Saint of the Twentieth Century*. London: Allen & Unwin, 1971.
Shaikh Aḥmad al-'Alawī. Contains wonderful descriptions of the doctrines and practices of a North African *ṭarīqa*.

———. *What is Sufism?* Allen & Unwin, 1975.
Outstanding description of what Sufism is about.

Macnab, Angus. *Spain Under the Crescent Moon*, chaps. 19, 20 and 21 on Andalusian Sufism.

Nasr, Seyyed Hossein. *Ideals and Realities of Islam:* Allen & Unwin, 1966.

———. *Sufi Essays:* Allen & Unwin, 1972.
Valuable discussions of many aspects of Sufism.

Nicholson, R. A. *The Mystics of Islam:* Routledge & Kegan Paul, 1975.
An excellent short survey, despite some doctrinal shortcomings.

Schimmel, Annemarie *Mystical Dimensions of Islam*: University of North Carolina Press, 1975.
Comprehensive historical survey. Though it is a little weak on the Maghrib, and rather uncritical regarding certain modern figures, it is a valuable and useful work.

Schuon, Frithjof. *Understanding Islam*. London: Allen & Unwin, 1963. Baltimore, Maryland: Penguin Books Inc., 1972.
Islam explained from a Sufi point of view.

———. *Dimensions of Islam*. London: Allen & Unwin, 1970.
A companion volume to 'Understanding Islam'. Fascinating chapters

on Sufi attitudes towards Christ and the Virgin Mary.

________. *Sufism: Veil and Quintessence*: World Wisdom Books, Bloomington, Indiana, 1981.

An enlightening comparison of historical and quintessential Sufism, with an outstanding chapter on the metaphysical teachings of the Arab philosophers.

B. Some translations of original Sufi writings

'Aṭṭār, Farīd ad-Dīn (twelfth century). *Muslim Saints and Mystics:* Routledge & Kegan Paul, 1966.
Extracts from the *Tadhkirat al-Auliyā* translated by A. J. Arberry.

ibn 'Arabī, Muḥyi 'd-Dīn (1165–1240). *Sufis of Andalusia:* Allen & Unwin, 1971.
The *Rūh al-quds* and extracts from the *Durrat al-fākhirah* translated by R. W. J. Austin.

ibn 'Aṭā' illāh (thirteenth century). *Sufi Aphorisms.* Leiden: Brill, 1973.
The *Kitāb al-Ḥikam* translated by Victor Danner.

Mulay al-'Arabī ad-Darqāwī (c. 1743–1823). *Letters of a Sufi Master*, translated by Titus Burckhardt. London: Perennial Books, 1969.
Spiritual advice of a most practical nature; helpful answers to everyday spiritual problems.

Rumi, Jalāl ad-Dīn (thirteenth century). *Discourses of Rumi.*
Translated by A. J. Arberry. London: John Murray, 1961.

C. Islamic Art

Since Islamic art – at once particular and universal – is like an outward crystallization of Sufism, the following copiously illustrated books are listed:

Burckhardt, Titus. *The Art of Islam: language and meaning.* London: World of Islam Festival Publishing Company, 1976.

Grube, Ernst. *The World of Islam.* London: Paul Hamlyn, 1966.

Lings, Martin. *The Quranic Art of Calligraphy and Illumination.* London: World of Islam Festival Publishing Company, 1976.

Rice, David Talbot. *Islamic Art.* London: Thames & Hudson, 1965.

du Ry, Carol J. *Art of Islam.* New York and London: Harry Abrams, Inc., 1970.

INDEX

Judaism, 22, 27
Junaid, Abu'l-Qāsim al-, 57
Junaidī *ṭarīqa*, 57

Ka'ba, 27, 32, 33, 63
kali-yuga (Dark Age), 50
Kelly, Bernard, 29
khalwa, 61, 66
Khurrqānī, Abū 'l-Ḥasan, 42
Konya, 57
kshatriyas, 23

Laila, 74, 76
Latin, 25
Lings, Martin, 56, 62, 74, 85
love, *see maḥabba*
Macnab, Angus, 85
Madhkūr (the Invoked), 67
maḥabba (love, charity), 47, 51–52, 64
Mahayana Buddhism, 21
maithuna (sexual union), 71
majlis (gathering), 60, 66
Majnūn, 76
Malaya, 22
mantra (sacred formula), 67
ma 'rifa (knowledge, gnosis), 48
Mary, the Virgin (Sayyidat-nā Maryam), 27, 34, 68–70, 74
Massignon, Louis, 25, 43
materia, 71
materialism, 36, 50
Maulawī *ṭarīqa*, 57, 60
Mecca, 25, 27, 31, 32
Medieval, 30, 31, 57, 60, 71
Messinesi, Aristide, 72
method, spiritual, Ch. 3
Mevlevi, *ṭarīqa*, 57, 60
Middle Ages, 30, 31, 57
miḥrāb (prayer niche), (Quranic symbolism of), 68–69
mind, 53
monastic orders, vows, 59
monks, 59
monotheism, 22, 23, 25, 27
morality, morals, 29, 53
Muḥammad, the Prophet, 25–27, 44, 54, 58, 61, 63, 70
Muḥyi 'd-Dīn ibn 'Arabī, 51, 52, 70, 83, 86
Mulay al-'Arabī ad-Darqāwī, 60, 86
Mumtaz Mahal, 51
muqaddam (representative of a shaikh), 66
murshid (spiritual guide), 54
music, 66
Muslim, 26
mutabarrikūn, 55
mysticism, *passim*, esp. Ch. 3
mythologies, Aryan, 22, 27

nafs (soul), 47, 63
Name, Divine, frontispiece, 65, 67
Naqshbandī *ṭarīqa*, 59
Nasr, Sayyed Hossein, 85
Natura, 71
Neo-Platonism, 43
New Testament (Gospels), 26, 34, 68
Nigeria, 36
Nirvana 23, 70
nominalism, 30
non-duality, 49
Nordic religion, 22
North American Indians, 22, 50

obedience, 59
O'Connor, Fr Patrick, 36
Omar, the Caliph, 34, 58, 61
Omar Khayyam, 35
orthodoxy, 28–29, 41–43
orthodoxy, Eastern, 22, 47, 67
Othman, the Caliph, 34, 58

Palamas, St Gregory, 47, 71
Pallis, Marco, 30
palm-tree (Quranic symbolism of), 68–69
pantheism, 49
Paul, St, 41, 67